Aunty Phil
Love Eileen & Mark
Josh
8/3/90

7

Aunty Phil
Love Eileen & Mark
Josh
8/3/90

Jack Thompson
DOWN UNDER

Jack Thompson
DOWN UNDER

Text by
Anne Matthews and Ray Sinclair

WELDON RUSSELL
PUBLISHING

Endpapers: *Irrigation is a way of life for fruit farmers in the Mildura area, Victoria.*
Leo Meier/Weldon Trannies

Page 1. *As dawn breaks across the horizon, two surfboard riders make their way towards the ocean.*
Guy Finlay/Weldon Trannies

Pages 2 and 3. *Aboriginal children bathe in a waterhole among the lush vegetation of the Northern Territory.*
Claire Leimbach

Pages 4 and 5. *Misty morning light filters through rainforest foliage.*
Carmen Ky

Opposite. *An outback day can be long, hot and hard. These drovers take a welcome break from riding.*
Weldon Trannies

Published by Weldon Russell Pty Ltd
372 Eastern Valley Way, Willoughby,
NSW 2068, Australia
A member of the Weldon International Group of Companies
In association with Great Southland Productions Pty Ltd

First published 1989

Editors: Christine MacKinnon, Nada Madjar
Picture Research: Carmen Ky
Design: Christie & Eckermann Art Design Studio, Sydney

National Library of Australia
Cataloguing-in-Publication Data

Jack Thompson down under.

Includes index.
ISBN 1 875202 04 8.

1. Australia — Description and travel — 1976–   . 2.
Australia — Social life and customs — 1976–   . 3.
Australia — Description and travel — 1976–   — Views. 4.
Australia — Social life and customs — 1976–   — Pictorial
works. I. Thompson, Jack, 1940–   . II. Sinclair, Ray.
III. Matthews, Anne. IV. Title: Jack Thompson down under
(Television program).

994.06'3

Typeset by Monoset Typesetters, Strathpine, Queensland.
Aaron Paul's Typesetting, Tempe, New South Wales.
Printed by The Griffin Press, Netley, S.A. Australia.

A KEVIN WELDON PRODUCTION

Foreword

My work takes me all over the world, to film locations as diverse as a scriptwriter's imagination. One country keeps drawing me back — Australia, my home. Despite the glamour and attraction of other countries and cultures, I always return with the knowledge that I live in one of the most fascinating and diverse places in the world.

Working on the television series *Jack Thompson Down Under* has provided me with the opportunity to express this fascination to the world. The program takes a many-faceted look at Australia, its unique people and places. It's not about flag-waving, but about a special sense of belonging to the land 'down under'.

My association with the program has also been a learning experience. I've come across all sorts of fascinating characters and unique aspects of Australian life — from the gaping jaws of a crocodile and the heat and dust of the outback, to the fast pace and sophistication of our modern cities.

For me, it was a chance to share in the courage and endurance of this land and its people; the adventure and excitement; the past and the future; the humour and the tragedy that are all an integral part of a unique way of life.

Now, the excitement and adventure of this land are brought to you in the book *Jack Thompson Down Under*. Drawing on the best of the television series, I believe this beautifully illustrated publication captures something of the essence of Australia and its people.

I believe that the television series and the book will help both Australians and our friends throughout the world to come to a greater understanding of our community and our great and unique wildlife and wilderness heritage. Perhaps this understanding will help us to better conserve this vital and diverse environment for our mutual benefit and that of generations to come.

I am proud to be associated with both the television series and the book. I hope you will receive as much enjoyment from these pages as I have had in bringing you a glimpse of the 'faces and places of the life down under'.

Contents

ACKNOWLEDGEMENTS 12

INTRODUCTION 13

ENVIRONMENT 19

Endangered Plants 20
Marine Life 24
Nullarbor 32
Christmas Island 38
Waiting for the Big Bang 41
Spirit of Olegas 46
Rainforest Communities 50
Sapphire 60

NATIVE FAUNA 63

Islands of the Moonbird 64
Whale Savers 69
Pygmy Possums 76
Secrets of Survival 80
Fairy Penguins 90
Underwater Communities 94
Numbats 104

ADVENTURE 111

Challenge of Lake Eyre 112
Shark Catchers 117
Quiet Challenge 121
Three Men in a Raft 124
Backyard Wings 130

Snowy Mountain Riders 134
The Drivers 139
Monte Cristo 146
Mystery of *Zanoni* 148
Eighteen Footers 152

CULTURE AND HISTORY 157

Peppimenarti 158
Every Dot Gently and Carefully 166
The Contract 172
Women of Utopia 174
The White Rose Orchestra 178
Educational Experiment 180
Billinudgel 187
Sunshine Man 190
The Women 194

PEOPLE 197

She Simply Wanted to Fly 198
Taipan Man 201
New Achievements 204
Surf Shaper 208
The Bear 214
Bogong High Plains 216
One Man's View 220
La Volpe 225
Master of His Trade 228
Young Tom 234
Marathon 236

INDEX 240

Opposite. *With spinnaker in full flight the yacht* Hitchhiker *dashes through the water.*

Acknowledgements

The publishers would like to acknowledge the kind assistance and advice of the following people: Mike O'Donoghue, Mrs J. Crocker, Tony Stokes and Jan Aldenhoven, John Hunter, Mrs Melva Truchanas, Geoff Richardson, Neal Bethune and Laurie Levy, Ken Shortman, Geoff Holloway, David Barton, John and Roma Dulhunty, John Hepworth, Ian Croll, Hans Litjens, John Weymouth, Frank Quealey, C. W. Riley, Reg Ryan, the Pendergast family, Bill Geoffrey, Glen Rogers and Lisa Voukolos, Daphne Williams, Rosalie Kunoth-Monks, Frank Bourke, John Greenslade, Spencer Jones, Frank Sims, Nancy-Bird Walton, Ram Chandra, Bob McTavish, Vicki Roycroft, Tor and Jane Holth, Jack Earl, Ian Braund, the Brown family, Graeme Hannan and Robert de Castella.

We would like to thank executive producers Matthew Flanagan and Mikael Borglund, Julie Miller and Ghita Fiorelli at 'Jack Thompson Down Under' for their valuable help in the compilation of this book and, also, Ross Wolrige (ABC Marketing), Robyn Watts (Film Australia Marketing and Distribution) and the producers and directors of Film Australia productions; Graham Chase, John Edwards, Keith Gow, Oliver Howes, Ron Iddon, Peter Johnston, Elizabeth Knight, Don Murray, Dennis O'Rourke, Timothy Read and Nick Torrens. Special thanks must go to Linda Christie, Joy Eckermann and their staff.

Introduction

Australia, 'the land down under', makes compelling television viewing. With its rich diversity of people and places, unique wildlife and ever-changing landscape, it has provided inspiration for many film makers, including some of the best documentary makers in the world.

'Jack Thompson Down Under' is a magazine-style television series which draws upon the libraries of excellent film footage. The program is a collection of stories about the Australian people and their environment, covering every aspect of life 'down under' and revealing Australia as a multi-faceted nation.

Jack Thompson, the host of the series, is one of Australia's leading actors. Jack has appeared in many award-winning feature films, both here and overseas, including *Breaker Morant, Merry Christmas Mr Lawrence, The Man from Snowy River, Sunday Too Far Away* and *Burke and Wills*. In 1986, he was awarded membership of the Order of Australia for his services to the film industry, and he is currently a director of the Australian Film Finance Corporation.

With his suntanned good looks and laconic manner, Jack typifies the Australian image, particularly in the United States where he has recently been seen in a number of prime time television dramas.

Although his career as an internationally recognised actor takes him to locations around the world, Jack is a permanent resident of Australia. His love for the country and its people is well known, and he actively promotes Australia's unique cultural heritage through his involvement with the National Museum in Canberra, which has one of the most comprehensive collections of Aboriginal art and artefacts in existence.

As a member of environmental groups such as the World Wildlife Fund and the Australian Conservation Foundation, Jack Thompson is perhaps one of Australia's best known and outspoken conservationists. He has narrated and presented documentaries about the delicate balance of Australia's environment, and was on the advisory committee for the publication *Australia's Wilderness Heritage*. His commitment to the preservation of our wildlife and environment was recently honoured with an invitation to address the 1989 International Conference on Environmental Law. This

MATTHEW FLANAGAN

year he has also been appointed the Goodwill Ambassador for the United Nations High Commission for Refugees — the first Australian to be thus honoured.

When Jack was approached to present the 'Down Under' series, the proposal was greeted with enthusiasm. Here was a chance for Jack not only to share his love and concern for Australia and its way of life, but also to promote the film industry of which he is such an integral part.

Jack's involvement was more than that of a studio narrator. Instead, he went 'bush', introducing each segment on location, bringing him closer to the people and atmosphere of the stories.

For weeks, Jack and a camera crew travelled throughout the countryside, experiencing all the extremes of Australia's climate first hand, from the tropical heat of northern Queensland to blizzards in the snow country. Dust, wind and torrential rain are just a part of filming in the great outdoors!

On occasions, Jack was asked to deliver his lines from places which would faze most people — such as a compound full of three metre saltwater crocodiles! Other less hazardous experiences included rounding up cattle on horseback in outback Queensland and exploring the wonders of the Great Barrier Reef.

Despite the apparent glamour associated with the film industry, the days on the road with the crew from 'Jack Thompson Down Under' were long and arduous. Filming began at dawn, and continued until last light. For Jack, there were countless takes to camera, lines to learn and wardrobe changes between endless locations.

Above and opposite. *Filming on location was often hazardous for actors, crew and photographic equipment, but some good friends were made along the way.*

Roland McManis, Paul Tait, Georgina Harrap and co-executive producer Mikael Borglund on location in the ski country of New South Wales. The crew experienced all the extremes of Australia's climate. from the tropical heat to the icy winds and blizzards.

Like Nancy-Bird Walton in her Gypsy Moth, Jack found that flying in an open-topped light plane was an exhilarating experience — matched only by the thrill of soaring in an ultra light glider.

BRENDAN READ

Co-executive producer Matthew Flanagan and Jack Thompson confer on details of the script.

Jack's experience as an actor and his familiarity with scripts were invaluable in the writing process. He continually conferred with the writers, discussing lines and often changing them into a language he felt more comfortable with.

Wherever the stories took them, the production team were made welcome, and Jack always found time to have a yarn with the townspeople and sign autographs for his fans.

The making of 'Jack Thompson Down Under' did not start and end on location, however. Back at home base in Sydney, work continued for over a year to produce the twenty-six hour-long episodes.

Soon the jigsaw of stories — those brief vignettes of Australiana — began to take shape as a unified whole. But first each segment underwent a complex post-production process — editing, mixing and compiling — the time-consuming details which turn raw material into final product.

The finishing touch was the music, reflecting the moods and passions of the land and its people. The catchy theme has been highly acclaimed and was nominated for Best Musical Score in the 1988 Penguin awards.

To produce a series like 'Jack Thompson Down Under' takes months of intensive work; to enjoy it takes just a few minutes. The series proved to be a huge success both in Australia and overseas, with nations as diverse as Sweden, the United States, Zimbabwe and Great Britain welcoming the opportunity to take an intimate look at the land 'down under'. The program can even be seen in Botswana.

Viewers who enjoyed the series can now relive its most memorable moments in print. Jack Thompson is proud to present this book as an accompaniment to the series. It serves as a permanent reminder of the great film makers who contributed to 'Jack Thompson Down Under', and of the vitality and diversity of Australia and its people.

JULIE MILLER

ENVIRONMENT

*Australia's unique environment is exemplified by her forests: their
conservation has been the subject of much controversy.*
GRANT DIXON/THE WILDERNESS SOCIETY

ENDANGERED PLANTS

WELDON TRANNIES

The unique wildflowers of Western Australia are so famous that visitors from all over the country flock to the southwest of the state each spring to view them. They travel by coach and by rail to view the riot of colour in all shades of the rainbow. Altogether there are about 8,000 flowering plants in Western Australia, many of which are indigenous. They include the widespread and colourful Proteaceae family, which encompasses dryandras, grevilleas and banksias; the delicate blue, yellow or scarlet of the genus *Leschenaultia*; and 500 species of Australia's national flower, the brilliant yellow wattle (genus *Acacia*). These spectacular wildflowers, shrubs and trees are high on the list of the state's many tourist attractions, but there are growing fears for their survival.

Farming is the greatest threat to Western Australia's flora. As land is cleared and farmed, the state's most beautiful natural assets are often damaged and destroyed. John Briggs, an expert on endangered species, agrees that farming is largely responsible: 'I believe there must be a balance between conservation and farming. I mean, obviously we have to eat, so there is a need for agricultural clearing and development, but not at the expense of all native flora.'

Farmers must be made aware that their properties need to contain and protect their flowering treasures. Don Williams is a sheep and wheat farmer whose land is in one of the state's most heavily vegetated areas. While clearing a section of his property, Don became curious about a particular stand of trees and hesitated in cutting

WELDON TRANNIES

Western Australia's unique range of wildflowers are a product of the State's isolation. The resulting 8,000 species have become Western Australia's famous attractions, but many of these plants are now endangered as land has gradually been cleared for farming.

Above. Brightly coloured flowers form a contrast to the stark landscape of the Stirling Ranges.

Right. An outback road is turned into a riot of yellow colour.

Opposite. There are several species of dryandra in the family Proteaceae, small trees with large flowers of various hues.

WELDON TRANNIES

them down. It was a prudent decision as the stand was a pocket of an extremely rare eucalypt species. However, as Don says, 'If I hadn't noticed it and persevered in asking botanists what its name was, it certainly could have been cleaned out.'

LEO MEIER/WELDON TRANNIES

Above and right. *With government information programs and preservation measures, farming and conservation may be able to coexist to ensure a future for beautiful plants such as the dryandra and the leschenaultia.*

Don agrees with John Briggs that farming and conservation can coexist, but Don has had to pay a price for saving his rare trees. He has fenced off the 8 hectares of trees, paid for the fencing himself and lost money by not farming the area. If saving a stand of rare eucalypts is of such importance to Don Williams, maybe other farmers will follow his example, and protect the endangered species on their land. It should not be left to chance—the state government must implement an information program to educate farmers on the importance of these plants and the necessity for their preservation.

Roadside verges are also in need of protection. Wild flowers and rare plants that have escaped the farmers' machinery often find refuge there, but even this home is no longer safe. Many plants are now under the threat of extinction from the practice of roadside clearing. A striking example of this is the red-flowered genus *Darwinia*. There are 33 species, of which 28 are confined to Western Australia.

In 1980, the Western Australian government decided that it was time to act—to save its rare plants and to protect certain roadside verges. But despite legislation introduced in 1980, the implementation of conservation measures can be costly and time-consuming. We can only hope that time does not run out, and that the government succeeds in saving plants like the genus *Darwinia* from joining the growing list of over 100 extinct and 200 endangered plant species.

TONY RODD/WELDON TRANNIES

MARINE LIFE

REG MORRISON/WELDON TRANNIES

The fishing rod is fully extended, and the bait jiggles invitingly from the end. Small fish circle curiously, but fail to rise to the lure. Perhaps they are not hungry, or perhaps some inner sense warns them of impending disaster. What they are avoiding, momentarily, is the astonishing food-catching device of one of the most bizarre of all marine animals, the angler fish. Its rod and bait are evolutionary extensions of its top fin, yet this is only one means it has of catching food.

The angler fish, a creature of Australia's reef waters, has evolved in almost every way. Water taken in through its gills is jet-propelled from openings at the base of its front fins. These fins have taken on the look, and action, of legs, or perhaps arms, with joints.

Having failed to lure its prey into its large mouth, the angler fish creeps forward in a series of excessively tiny movements, walking across the seabed, over small rocks, inexorably towards its prey.

Nobody knows whether it hypnotises its prey or exudes some kind of chemical, but the result is swift and satisfying. The angler creeps within close proximity of a fish that dares not look away and seems unable to flee until the very last moment. Then it is too late. The

Australia's marine life is incredibly varied and colourful.

Above. *A tube anemone.*
Opposite. *A diver pauses to study feather starfish.*

JEAN-PAUL FERRERO/AUSCAPE INTERNATIONAL

incredibly patient angler suddenly strikes, taking only a fraction of a second to envelop and swallow its prey.

To find an angler fish in Australian waters is to discover just one example of many remarkable steps in the evolutionary process. One of the simplest forms of marine life is probably the sea anemone, which is little more than a reflexing bundle of jelly. It consists of only two layers of cells, it cannot see or hear, and it catches its food by accident.

Corals, too, are primitive, but finding their food is even more of a fortunate accident, as they are immobile. The tiny polyps colonise to form corals culminating in large structures the size of the Great Barrier Reef, providing food and shelter for many small fish.

One cell layer bigger than the coral polyp is the flatworm, which has a more complex nervous system. Flatworms are free-moving and have eye spots and special cells to inform them of their surroundings.

Molluscs have developed mobile homes: solid, lightweight shells that defend their soft bodies. Gastropods, like the algae-grazing sea hare, have virtually discarded the shell and rely on camouflage and slow movement to keep them out of a predator's sights.

Many tiny creatures offer visions of remarkable beauty. Even though one bears the unflattering name of batwing sea slug, it travels, or flees danger, by poising delicately before launching itself upwards in a flutter of delicate pink 'wings' looking more like a rainforest butterfly than a slug.

Above. *The brightly coloured striated angler fish (*Antennarius striatus*) uses an unusual method to catch its food. It creeps towards the prey and eventually stuns it—perhaps by the release of a chemical—and swallows it in a fraction of a second.*

Right. *Hard and soft corals add colour to the submarine scenery.*

Overleaf. *This red coral fan is one of many varieties of coral.*
I. R. MARRINER/WELDON TRANNIES

I. R. MARRINER/WELDON TRANNIES

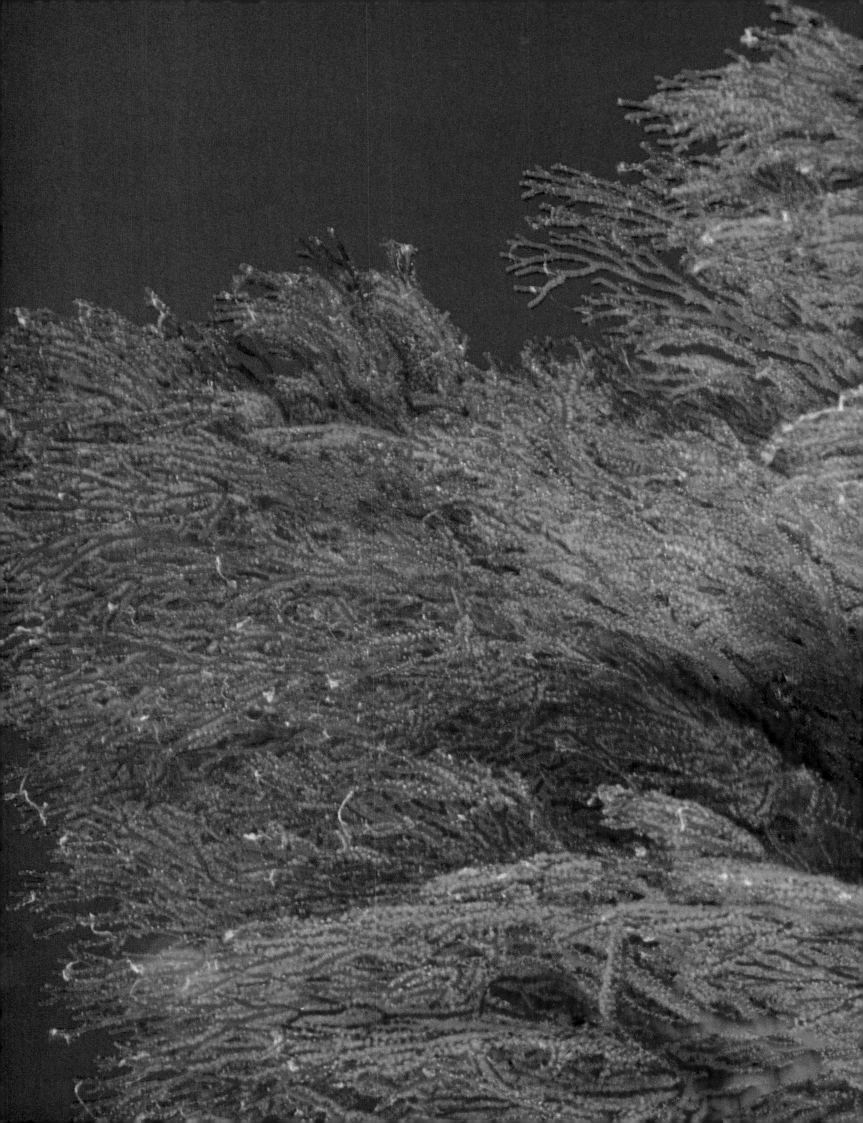

D. PARKER & E. PARKER-COOK/AUSCAPE INTERNATIONAL

The sea slug (Cyerce nigricans) is yet another brightly coloured and strange ocean creature. These animals have no protective shell to cover their soft bodies, but protect themselves with an unpleasant tasting sticky substance which coats their skin. They can also repel potential predators by releasing a chemical irritant.

The true sea slugs, or nudibranchs, have soft bodies and are not protected by the vestigial shell of the gastropods. Instead they are covered with a sticky foul-tasting slime that does not invite a second lick. They also release a chemical irritant. Certain of the power of their repellants, they deliberately advertise their inviolability by displaying themselves in brilliant coloured spots of orange and yellow, or black bodies with white dots.

Camouflage for the decorator crab seems more rooted in vanity than necessity—but that, of course, is from a human point of view. Yet it is difficult not to recognise certain human foibles in the time-consuming care with which the decorator delicately plucks coral, seaweed and rocks to attach, item by item, to its shell. Even living coral is transplanted, till the decorator is indistinguishable from its surroundings. It all begins again as the crab sheds its shell on regular occasions.

The feather star is possibly the oldest starfish; its long, branching arms transport food from branch to branch through sticky mucus to a mouth above the body. The brittle star has developed a mouth underneath; and the biscuit star, which is more familiar,

MIKE TINSLEY/AUSCAPE INTERNATIONAL

There are a number of varieties of starfish which are familiar throughout Australian waters, but the feather star is quite different. This variety has long feathery arms which wave gracefully in the water, and are used to transfer food to the mouth, through a sticky mucous substance.

has stubbier arms and a body that looks as though it is tiled in red and pink.

When a starfish damages an arm, it can replace it, but the surprise to those of us who see it as the living representation of the classic five-point star of the skies is that the creature will often grow several legs where one has been lost.

The tiny and much-loved seahorse evolved to take advantage of places not already overcrowded. Like miniature mediaeval knights, they quietly anchor their tails to seaweed, graze gently, then flutter their back fin in fairy tale fashion to another field of weed.

The octopus represents one of the most advanced forms of marine life. It is related to oysters and snails, but a simple experiment illustrates its amazing intelligence. A jar, filled with seawater and a little crab, is sealed with a screw-top lid and placed near an octopus hole. Within a few moments, the octopus emerges, unscrews the lid, and removes its favourite delicacy. Though slow the first time, the octopus becomes faster the second time. If you find it hard to believe, try it yourself.

NULLARBOR

Exploration of the Nullarbor plain was carried out for the same reason as most other early Australian explorations. The still young colony needed agricultural and grazing land, but while the evidence always showed aridity, men still dreamed of undiscovered waterways.

In 1840, Edward John Eyre travelled the 3,200 kilometre (2,000 mile) journey from Adelaide to Albany—and became the first white man to do so. Eyre was honoured for his courage, but he had discovered nothing of more than geographical interest.

Thirty years later, John Forrest set out from the western end, determined to find 'the river' he believed Eyre had missed. Five months later, in Adelaide, he was to confirm the apparent uselessness of the waterless, treeless desert.

Australians now speed across the Nullarbor in the comfort of the Indian Pacific train, or air-conditioned cars and coaches on a sealed road. They know it is called the Eyre Highway, and they note with little interest a tiny Nullarbor outpost named Forrest. Their abiding impression is similar to that of the explorers; that the Nullarbor is empty of interest.

Closer scrutiny proves otherwise. The 'no tree' plain is a land of surprises. Perhaps the first surprise was for Eyre himself. At one stage during his journey, he staggered from the burning flatness of the plain to what must have seemed the edge of the world. He found the sheer cliffs of the Great Australian Bight, terminating the Nullarbor in an abrupt, dizzying 400 metre drop. Eyre was stunned.

Forrest later had the same experience. He reported: 'After looking very cautiously over the precipice, we all ran back quite terror-stricken by the dreadful view.'

While Europeans gave this land the Latin name meaning 'no tree', the Aborigines have always called it 'Oondeerie', which means 'waterless'. Yet there is plant life and water there.

Anyone crossing the Nullarbor after spring rains will never forget a desert carpeted with wildflowers whose seeds have waited patiently to burst through the generally parched earth. As for water, there is Queen Victoria Springs. It sounds grand but the monarch's name falls upon only a tiny, muddy bog discovered by Tommy, an Aborigine travelling with the expedition of Ernest Giles. The waterhole may not have been of regal proportions, but it saved the lives of Giles, his five expeditioners and their camels. One tiny waterhole in a desert that stretches 800 kilometres across the bottom of Australia, and 350 kilometres north from those terrifying but magnificent cliffs of the Bight is not much to recommend the area, yet the pioneering spirit remains—people continue to be challenged by it.

WELDON TRANNIES

Above. Early explorers tackled the unmapped Nullarbor with grit and determination.
Opposite. *The first Nullarbor travellers were stunned to discover the dramatic drop from the plain to the sea.*
Overleaf. *The desert: rocks, red earth and scrub.*
LEO MEIER/WELDON TRANNIES

The well-known, well-loved Daisy Bates came to the desert to Ooldea—to care for Aborigines. For 16 years during the early 1900s she lived in a tent, always wearing her heavy, Victorian clothes. When she died, she was immortalised in Aboriginal Dreamtime as Kabbarli—the Grandmother.

Other people came to the Nullarbor, too. Railway people came to maintain the trans-Australian railway. It boasts the longest straight stretch of track in the world— 530 kilometres—a silvery line across a vast land, and still the railway workers cluster together like big city suburbanites in their little houses seeking security from the emptiness around them.

One of the earliest attempts at settlement came with the need for communication and the establishment of the Overland Telegraph. A little settlement sprang up on the South Australian–Western Australian border—a triumph of bureaucracy, even in this isolation. People worked in both States, handing the telegraphed messages through a porthole marking the border. Actually, it was a lively settlement of 300 people, 90 of whom were postal workers, their wives and children. They enjoyed race meetings, cricket, tennis and death-adder hunts in the years between 1880 and 1927, but the only traces remaining today are crumbling sandstone walls jutting jaggedly from the ever-shifting, relentlessly consuming white sands.

Crossing the Nullarbor, the slower traveller may come across a lone rabbiter, making a little money while also going a small way towards protecting the shifting, fragile environment from the introduced animals that eat the tussocks binding the dunes.

At Balladonia, site of the 'last rock before the Nullarbor begins' on the western side, an elderly lady named Mrs Crocker shows a painting of Afghan cameleers watering their animals, and recalls that 'Such areas could not have existed without them.' She lives on her property with an eye on Big Red Rock and will talk for hours about the insects and other colourful life of the so-called desert. 'People just do not stop to look,' she says of the speeding cars that now cross the once-great barrier with such ease.

The explorers had little time to appreciate the charms of the Nullarbor. They were concerned only with survival. Perhaps John Forrest, who had battled from west to east for five months, gained a better appreciation of the desert beauty when he stepped aboard the first train in 1917 to cross the Nullarbor, this time, in only three days.

There is something about the Nullarbor that is eternal. Maybe it is Jidara. For thousands of years, Aborigines believed Jidara came from the sea to the great plain. The roaring wind rising from blowholes in the massive limestone bed of the plain is the breath of Jidara, threatening to devour intruders. Only recently, explorers were trapped by floods and cave-ins in these blowholes. Years ago, Aborigines believed that the first

great black hissing steam engine was Jidara, coming to eat them.

The train may not have been Jidara, but one could imagine his spirit in another human assault on the Nullarbor—at Maralinga, the atomic testing ground where the British experimented with controversial and destructive nuclear weapons that gave off blinding light and a fearsome roar.

When the lights of these many suns finally dimmed and the roars died, only the poisoned breath of the monsters remained to creep into unfortunate bodies, silently devouring them. Was this Jidara, the feared and respected monster of the Dreamtime, or a far more terrifying beast come to destroy indiscriminately?

The Nullarbor holds many secrets. Take your time and discover them. Marvel at the courage of those who first challenged this land. Experience the same shock as Eyre and Forrest, standing above those stunning cliffs where it all begins and ends so dramatically.

Above. *The flat and treeless Nullarbor plateau drops sharply into the Great Australian Bight.*
Opposite. *Although the Nullarbor is for the most part a dry, arid and often stony desert where few people would choose to live, there is life here. After rain, the desert blooms with wildflowers which transform the monotonous landscape into a blaze of colour.*

CHRISTMAS ISLAND

Christmas Island, a remnant of a volcano jutting out of the Indian Ocean, has, over thousands of years, become a lush tropical paradise. It was discovered by a passing British ship on Christmas Day 1615, but it remained undisturbed by people until 1888 when it was formally annexed by Great Britain.

Britain was anxious to exploit the mountain of phosphate created by Christmas Island's bird population. As digging continued, plants and wildlife took second place to the need for phosphate. Labourers were often treated as badly as the environment. Indentured labourers were brought from Malaya, branded like cattle for identification, and set to work mining the phosphate. The system continued until the 1930s.

The island was occupied by the Japanese during the Second World War, during which time many residents were evacuated. After the war, Christmas Island again came under British control until 1958 when it became an Australian territory.

Phosphate was mined for almost a hundred years. Demand kept diggers tearing away at the island for its economic riches, blatantly ignoring the riches of nature. The island's permanent labour force earned one-third of the Australian rate of pay. Australians, on the other hand, received good wages with bonuses such as freedom from taxation and the provision of a good standard of housing to compensate for their isolated life.

By the early 1980s, world phosphate prices had

For one hundred years, Christmas Island's economy depended on the mining of phosphate, which was transported from wharves such as the ones at Flying Fish Cove, the main township on the island.

JAN ALDENHOVEN

A. G. WELLS/AUSTRALIAN MUSEUM

JAN ALDENHOVEN

J. HICKS/AUSTRALIAN MUSEUM

This Pacific island has a large population of rare birds which have, over many years, created the phosphate.
Top left. A red-tailed tropic bird.
Top right. The Christmas Island hawk-owl.
Above. The greater frigate bird.

JAN ALDENHOVEN

JAN ALDENHOVEN

declined along with demand. Restructuring of the industry became necessary to avoid massive economic losses.

Environmental concerns were also raised. Christmas Island is home to many rare species of bird. The red-tailed tropic bird and the Christmas Island frigate bird, together with over 1,000 pairs of Abbott's booby, which are found only on this island, were threatened by mining operations, especially if the central plateau with its 8,000 birds nests was disturbed. Tony Stokes, a Canberra wildlife officer, described it as 'the equivalent of the Pacific Ocean's Galapagos'. Tony prepared to battle against the spread of mining: 'It is up to the government to decide if the future of the birds is more important than the limited phosphate resources remaining on the island.'

The government has introduced new conservation laws to protect the wildlife, but there is still much to be done if the rare species on this island are to have a chance of survival.

Above. *The Christmas Island red crab migrates annually from its forest home to breed in the sea.*
Left. *Young red crabs. The island has a large variety of unusual wildlife which was threatened by phosphate mining, but new conservation laws have been introduced.*

WAITING FOR THE BIG BANG

STEPHEN NUTT/WELDON TRANNIES

The beautiful beaches and lagoons of Papua New Guinea's seismologically active Rabaul are deceptively tranquil.

'We interrupt this program for an urgent newsflash on the volcanic situation . . . an eruption is now expected to break out within days or even hours.' The radio announcer's delivery carried an urgency to match the words that echoed around the deep-sheltered harbour city of Rabaul, at the northeastern end of New Britain Island, Papua New Guinea. He went on to a declaration of Stage Four Alert, with an order for immediate evacuation, and then finished with the statement: 'This is an exercise.'

At the time, the announcer was not being overly dramatic. The 95,000 inhabitants of this part of Papua New Guinea had every scientific reason to believe they were directly threatened by the kind of natural holocaust that had, ironically, given birth to the harbour.

According to evidence, the first volcanic eruption occurred in 1500 BC, followed by numerous eruptions over the next 2,000 years. During the last one in 1937, a small island erupted and one million tonnes of mud and ash crushed the beautiful garden city.

Rabaul is one of the most seismologically active areas on Earth. While the town is actually built in the crater resulting from the original eruptions, the most recent threat came from the movement of two great continental plates under the harbour. Between the early 1970s and 1984, the floor of the central part of the bay moved and the shoreline at the southern end of the Matupit Island in the centre of the bay rose by 1.8 metres. United Nations experts found a complete underwater volcano.

The year of greatest concern was 1984, when seismological evidence indicated a strong possibility of an eruption. Nobody knew what the future of Rabaul would be. The country's vulcanologist, Benjamin Talai, said that everybody was waiting for the coming eruption. 'It is not a question of if an eruption will happen, but a question of when.'

Benjamin is responsible for close and continual monitoring of all the signs. He remembers the 1937 eruption that killed five hundred people, and is fully aware of how important it is to avert the repetition of that disastrous event. One of his indicators of an eruption is a hot spring area which the invading Japanese of the Second World War used when they built bath houses. Any significant change in the temperature is likely to be a signal of trouble.

For Benjamin Talai and his colleague Nason Paulius, former chairman of the Provincial Disaster Committee, the major problem is always loss of interest. After false alarms, the people lose the sense of urgency necessary for their survival when a major disaster occurs. Emergency exercises are a help.

Rabaul is built on a crater which resulted from volcanic eruptions and is surrounded by extinct volcanoes such as this one. The major threat to the town's existence is movement from the two vast continental plates which meet underneath Rabaul's harbour. No one knows when the next Big Bang will occur.

STEPHEN NUTT/WELDON TRANNIES

STEPHEN NUTT/WELDON TRANNIES

STEPHEN NUTT/WELDON TRANNIES

Although the people of Rabaul live under the constant threat of volcanic eruption, they go about their daily business unperturbed.

Opposite:
Top. *Locals attend the daily markets.*
Bottom. *Fishermen cruise the lagoon waters in their canoes.*

Overhanging trees are cut back from escape routes, and streets are widened. Delays in the expected moment of genuine eruption have given Rabaul breathing space—time to set emergency procedures and safeguards in place to help people survive. Rabaul is regarded as perhaps the best-prepared seismologically active area in the world.

Yet the people readily slip back into their easy-going ways. Even the all-time record of more than 1,700 earthquakes which struck Rabaul on Easter Day in 1984 did not leave a lasting impression. The people of Rabaul have learned to live with insecurity to a point where many officials believe that the complacency is dangerous. At the height of the last alert, for example, Nason Paulius sent his family to a designated safe area—out of a comfortable home into a dirt floor grass hut shelter. Although there was a 90 per cent chance of a massive eruption, his family was not worried about the earthquake but was concerned with having to put up with poor emergency conditions.

Families living closer to the crater, however, admit they are scared. 'If it comes up suddenly, then we will lose our lives,' said one woman. A man added: 'We were told that we will have plenty of warning, but who knows? Something might come up in a minute or tomorrow. This is something that is uncertain and it is a worrying position.'

United Nations and Papua New Guinean scientists know the greatest threat comes from beneath the waters of Rabaul's deep circular harbour. The challenge is to use science to overcome the local belief, according to which an eruption happens only once every lifetime and the gods will advise people of the time and the place. The challenge is also to read the scientific auguries with a skill that will mean survival for the people of Rabaul, who are waiting for the Big Bang.

SPIRIT OF OLEGAS

Southwestern Tasmania is one of the most beautiful, rugged and untouched corners of our country, with nearly 13,000 square kilometres of deep, rocky gorges, fast flowing streams, dramatic waterfalls, tranquil lakes and ancient trees. It is a bushwalkers' paradise where virtually no roads, houses or people intrude. Much of it is now under the care of Department of Lands, Parks and Wildlife (formerly the National Parks and Wildlife Service), but this has not always been the case. Most of what we have now has been the result of long and hard-fought conservation battles.

People of vision have, for many years, fought governments and developers to save this unique wilderness and preserve its beauty for future generations to see and enjoy. There has been no-one with more vision and determination than an early pioneer of the Tasmanian conservation movement—Olegas Truchanas. Born in Lithuania, Olegas escaped war-torn Europe to settle in Tasmania. Required to work in whatever job he was allocated by the government of the day, Olegas found himself with a depressing, soul-destroying job in a Hobart electrolytic zinc works. As an escape, Olegas began to explore the countryside of his new home. He also indulged in his passion for photography, an art he had learned in the mountains of Europe.

He was drawn towards the southwest of Tasmania. Its wildness amazed and thrilled him, and as he penetrated further and further into this inaccessible and little-trodden country, his deep love and concern for the land increased. His solitary explorations included the climb of the previously elusive Federation Peak, and the use of the rivers to reach regions that he could not fully explore on foot.

The wild Gordon River had never been fully navigated by a European, and Olegas was determined to try. As the river was dangerous, and at points unnavigable, he built a special canoe which could be dismantled and carried over the rocky outcrops blocking his course. His first attempt failed when he was swept over a 6-metre waterfall and the canoe was pinned by the current to a midstream rock, but, undaunted, he succeeded on his second attempt, three years later.

Olegas continued his love affair with southwest Tasmania but destiny changed this solitary wanderer into a man with a mission, and a leading light of the conservation movement. One of Olegas's most loved parts of the southwest, Lake Pedder, was threatened with inundation by the damming of the Gordon River. Olegas was outraged and indignant over the proposed destruction of this beautiful stretch of water, and horrified by the lack of concern that Australians showed for preserving their own environment. Ironically, he could not speak out in public, because as an employee

Olegas Truchanas, the pioneer of Tasmania's conservation movement.

Opposite. *The beautiful Gordon River which winds its way through Tasmania's wilderness. Olegas was the first European to navigate the river's wild upper reaches and it always held a special fascination for him. It was on the Gordon that he disappeared during a photographic mission.*

of the Hydroelectric Commission he was bound to silence. Unable to fight the scheme verbally, he turned to another weapon. Pictures tell their own story and Olegas's photographic ability was put to best use in combating the government's proposals.

The bushfires of 1967 sadly destroyed his home, and he lost an irreplaceable collection of thousands of slides, including many of Lake Pedder. Determination sent Olegas back to the lake with his camera and he took new photographs—a wonderfully evocative series which captured the remoteness and beauty of this threatened wilderness. People saw his eloquent pictures and were inspired to see the lake for themselves, but though Olegas raised conservation consciousness and sparked off determined protests, it was too late to stop the flooding. His fight achieved an increased public awareness, but another challenge was yet to come.

OLEGAS TRUCHANAS

Olegas' most successful battle was to save 1000-year-old Huon pine trees on the Denison River. The forest was eventually designated as the Truchanas Huon Pine Reserve.

Opposite. Without reafforestation, logging can cause severe soil degradation and erosion. The hills around Queenstown, Tasmania, were laid bare by the demand for timber to fuel copper smelters and mine furnaces in the early 1900s. Bushfires and sulphur-dioxide fumes prevented any regeneration and resulted in devastating soil loss.

The Gordon River that Olegas had navigated years before was now under threat from a proposed dam. Apart from the changes this dam would bring to the river, Olegas believed it would give the tree cutters access to a unique area, endangering the world's last stand of 1,000-year-old Huon pines. Olegas was determined to win this battle. Despite fierce opposition, Olegas Truchanas and his growing band of conservationists won a hard-fought victory. The upstream forest, declared a reserve, is now officially gazetted as the Truchanas Huon Pine Reserve.

With one victory came another battle. The Gordon River was still threatened and so Olegas planned another photographic mission, one that was even more important to him than the Lake Pedder project. Olegas knew that another canoe trip on the Gordon would be dangerous, but by now he was obsessed, and more concerned with this mission than for himself. The long disputes had aged and tired him, and even he admitted that saving the Gordon would always be an uphill fight,

but his compulsion sent him back to the river, with canoe and camera, alone. Olegas Truchanas has never been seen since.

Olegas' death was a tragic loss, but it was fitting that the river he loved and fought for finally claimed him. His memorial is a greater awareness of what we might have lost, and an inspired conservation movement which still continues to fight his battles.

In Olegas' own words, 'The natural world contains an unbelievable diversity and offers a variety of choices. ... We must try to retain as much as possible of what still remains of the unique and beautiful. ... We don't know what the requirements of those who come after us will be. Tasmania is slowly evolving towards goals we cannot see ... if we can accept a role of steward and depart from the role of conqueror, if we can accept the view that man and nature are inseparable parts of the unified whole—then Tasmania can be a shining beacon in a dull and largely artificial world' (*The World of Olegas Truchanas*, 1975). Olegas' light still shines.

RAINFOREST COMMUNITIES

From the air, Australia's rainforests are a beautiful sight—a seemingly impenetrable, dense canopy of green. It is hard to imagine that anything, even sunlight, could pierce this choked profusion of growth; or that there could be such abundance of wildlife in its tangled foliage. If anyone cares to take a closer look, however, they will find an astonishing variety of plants, birds, animals and insects, thriving in an environment that supports more living things than any other region on Earth.

In the damp green rainforest every living thing has a purpose. Everything is interdependent and mutually reliant—a part of a hierarchy and a delicate balance which nature has evolved. Here in the rainforest, the trees are the unchallenged kings of that hierarchy. While small ferns compete with those plants that have developed glossy, broad leaves to prevent competitors from growing underneath them, none can compete with the trees. These tall giants stretch upwards to receive the full strength of life-giving sunlight, while the plants far below have to make do with a more filtered form. The big trees are determined to survive and have evolved ways of doing so.

The huge strangler fig (*Ficus watkinsiana*) which dominates many parts of the rainforest is one example. It makes an almost unnoticed entrance into the ecosystem. Initially, a fruit-eating bird might drop a seed onto the forest floor, where the roots sent out by the seed take hold and grow so strong that the new tree 'strangles' the host which it has adopted and used for its own support.

Trees play a positive role in the rainforests, for without them much of the forest's life would disappear. Apart from the need for light, the growth of so many plants in such a densely packed area is dependent on

The rainforest supports an extraordinary variety of life. The trees stretch upwards in search of light, preventing full light reaching the undergrowth.

Opposite. *Some ferns and vines attach themselves to the trunks of massive trees so that they can obtain more light.*

LEO MEIER/WELDON TRANNIES

Top left. *Flying foxes, of which there are four known species in Australia, feed on fruit or blossoms, whichever is the most abundant at the time.*
Top right. *The brush turkey remains on the ground during the day but at night it roosts in the trees.*
Above and opposite. *The incredible lushness of a northern rainforest.*
Overleaf. *The Daintree is one of Australia's most famous rainforests.*

Among the often dense forest live many small creatures, such as this frog, which are a part of the rich variety of the rainforest environment.

Previous page. A forest fire in Queensland's Daintree region. The building of a road into the Daintree rainforest prompted enormous public debate on the conservation of Australia's wilderness areas.

water, and trees play a vital part in this life-giving cycle. The forest's high canopy enables water to drip constantly and filter through, until it eventually reaches even the smallest and most delicate plants far below. The forest floor also benefits. The rainwater which is not soaked up immediately by the soil is left to carry a vital food supply, in the form of chemicals, throughout the forest. In turn, this excess rainwater helps to break down the compost of fallen leaves, thus benefiting the tiny fungi which thrive in this moist forest carpet.

As well as the trees and plants that make up the rainforest's rich variety of life, birds, insects, frogs, beetles and snakes such as the rainforest python live in this lush environment and are all links in the chain of coexistence. The giant snail (*Hedleyella folconeri*), for

example, eats the fungi which have grown out of the forest's compost, and in doing so the snail passes on, in its own small way, the broken down tree waste to the rest of the forest. The flying fox (or fruit bat), of which there are four known species in Australia, also has a role to play. In carrying seeds across the forest on its foraging flights, it drops some and thus becomes a link in the pollination process. The red-headed brush turkey (*Alectura lathami*) is dependent on the trees in a rather different way. Once the eggs have been laid, the male turkey scratches up dead leaves to cover them. The resulting heat incubates his mate's eggs. The male's head is heat sensitive and he can adjust the heat of the nest by the removal or addition of the precious leaves that the trees have provided. It is another example of the

H. & J. Beste/Australian Museum

Many snakes are well adapted to life in the rainforest, using the trees as their habitat. They are often the same deep green colour as the plants and trees around them.

rainforest's interdependence, and one that, again, starts and ends with trees. They are the forest's most vital link in the life-giving cycle. Removal causes chaos.

Humankind's need and passion for timber does not only remove trees; it also disturbs the balance that nature has so carefully evolved. The life of a rainforest begins and ends with its trees. During the early 1800s, trees were an essential factor in the country's growth—rosewood, cedar and coachwood were all excellent building materials. Then settlers began to clear the land for farming, and the indiscriminate removal of the forests gained momentum. After the mid-1800s more than half of Australia's rainforests were felled to create beef and dairy farmland. Although they had the land, farmers soon began to realise, alas too late, that the damage had been

done. Without the trees, the topsoil was destabilised and was washed away in heavy rains. As a result, the soil lost much of its richness and ability to soak up rainwater, and the farmland thus lost much of its value.

At last mankind has realised that the removal of these trees, and indeed entire rainforests, affects the environment with a totality and finality previously unimagined. It has been estimated that it would take at least two hundred years to regenerate a decimated rainforest—a chilling fact indeed. It is obvious that such forests are not only the oxygen-giving lungs of the world, but also that the plants and animals that shelter within them depend for their very life on the survival of the forests.

SAPPHIRE

AUSTRALIAN BROADCASTING CORPORATION

In the harsh and stony land of central Queensland squats a crude settlement with no apparent reason for existing. Sapphire is the name of this desolate spot and the secret of its existence. This is a sapphire-mining town.

The unattractively pitted and pimpled surface of Sapphire is a chart of youthful hopes and dreams. Each little hole, each pile of stony soil is testimony to someone's desire for beauty and wealth. It is also testimony to the hard work of the miners, who are known at times to employ the simplest of methods in mining the world's fourth most precious gemstone—sapphire!

The miners mostly come with their small young families, are single people or are elderly Australians. Many of them live in the simplest of shanties, yet their combined output of sapphires provides three-quarters of the world's supply.

Ron and Jan Sky are a couple of such miners. Ron and Jan came as tourists, found a couple of gemstones, and stayed. Sapphire mining, says Ron, 'is not just a job. It is a way of life.' The shanty in which they live is located on their 30 metre square claim, with the shaft only six metres away. Ron works until he is exhausted. He explains, 'You know, you pull a nice, fancy stone out of here and feel that it is worth going down there and doing more digging. You're dying to get back down the shaft to see what you are going to get out next.'

Above. *The small, rugged Queensland settlement of Sapphire attracts a variety of hopeful gem prospectors.*

Opposite.
Top. *Sapphires in their natural and polished states.*
Bottom. *A sapphire miner works in the cramped confines of his mine.*

REG MORRISON/WELDON TRANNIES

All a miner like Ron Sky needs is a miner's right, a permit to scavenge and $150 to register a claim. The basic equipment needed is a car to get there, a trailer to bring in a couple of 44-gallon drums of water to wash the gravel with, a tripod with a sieve to sift and wash the stones in, and a pick and a shovel.

The formulation of sapphire gems began with the prehistoric eruptions of the volcanoes located in this area. Tiny lava droplets became buried to begin the metamorphosis into the blue, green and yellow treasures mined today.

While highly-publicised gold rushes came and went, the sapphire seekers went quietly about their scavenging for one hundred years. Now, sapphires are a multi-billion dollar business. Inevitably, the big companies realised the profits to be made from this industry, and moved in with their bulldozers. Vast areas of land were pushed up and probed. Power became the 'open sesame' to Aladdin's cave and bitter feuds erupted. Guns were often pulled, accompanied by the classic line: 'Shoot first and ask questions later.'

The Queensland government finally stepped in. Certain areas were ceded to the giant earth-movers, while others were confined to the smaller operators. There was still some antagonism and resentment, but the smaller operators felt time was on their side, because high costs of large-operation mining and lower prices of sapphires would drive the big companies away and leave them to their one-man shafts.

One of the small operators is a grizzled old fellow who resembles the typical lone miner. He is Brickie Hays, who has been coming to Sapphire for more than twenty years. Brickie makes a living from sapphires, but only barely. Another miner did find one of the biggest yellow stones only a couple of metres away but Brickie is still scratching for that elusive prize. He says, however, that he never gets tired of mining. 'That is the best part of it,' he explains, 'taking chances all the time; whether you're gonna get the big one or miss altogether.'

Not everyone in Sapphire is, however, a pick-and-shovel miner. Ian Flavell came nearly thirty years ago to cut and polish the gems but now his former workshop is a dusty, cobwebbed relic of the days when he was sought out as one of the best cutters in the country. These days Ian spends most of his time as a motor mechanic, helping to fix the crude screening plants when they break down. The stones he used to handle with skill and love now go to cutters in Thailand.

Thailand, itself a producer of sapphires, dominates the market. To maintain their hold, the Thais locate their buyers among the shacks of Sapphire, taking 99 per cent of the Australian stones. Though Australians pay thirty or forty times their original value, they are our own treasures, having done the round trip to and from Bangkok, where cheap labour allows the gems to be cut for about 40 cents (rather than $12) per carat.

Nothing, however, can draw the 'little diggers' away from the scarred landscape they call home. It is a peaceful place to chase their dreams, or simply relax and enjoy the thrill of a small but beautiful find. When they have to defend themselves, they will, as in the earlier battle with big company technology. When a pick-and-shovel miner found an operator gouging a huge hole near his shaft, he was enraged: 'I raced down with a rifle and put a shot just through the top of his hat.' He then told him to fill the hole in. The operator complied.

One man behind the big operations is Ray Richardson. He lives in a sprawling, comfortable home and he does not use a pick or shovel. Ray says, 'Sapphires, as far as I am concerned, are just rock. They are just a means of making money.' Ron Sky and his neighbours in the pits and trenches cannot understand Ray's attitude. Ron believes he can recognise his own stones anywhere. He says that 'each one almost has a pet name.'

AUSTRALIAN BROADCASTING CORPORATION

NATIVE FAUNA

*The jewel beetle (family Buprestidae) is one of Australia's
colourful and varied native creatures.*

JAN ALDENHOVEN

ISLANDS OF THE MOONBIRD

C. HAAGER/AUSTRALIAN MUSEUM

In the windswept and treacherous waters of Bass Strait lies an intriguing rugged group of forty-two islands—the Islands of the Moonbird—that make up the Furneaux group. These hilly patches of land encompass peaks that are an extension of the Great Dividing Range, which winds its way down Australia's eastern flank. Ten thousand years ago, the islands were joined to the mainland as part of a long bridge, but now the gales of the notorious roaring forties region whip the waters that separate the islands from the continent into a maelstrom that has claimed many ships and countless lives.

Situated off the northeast tip of Tasmania, the islands were reached in 1773 by Tobias Furneaux, the captain of Cook's support ship, *Adventure*, which became separated from the main fleet and sailed down the coast of Van Diemen's Land. Aborigines named the islands after the moonbird, better known as the muttonbird or short-tailed shearwater (*Puffinus tenuirostris*), believing that the birds were made homeless after the moon fell off the earth.

These birds are the islands' biggest attraction. Muttonbirds have long been hunted for their tasty meat and their oil, which has medicinal uses. Each September,

the birds migrate from Japan and the Bering Strait to settle in burrows to lay their eggs. When the adults leave in April, the mutton-birders arrive to hunt the young.

British, French and American sailors also came to cull the once-abundant seal population, and many of the islanders today are descendants of these unruly sealer gangs of the early 1800s. Tragically, this once widespread activity wiped out the hair seal, and the present fur seal population was once almost extinct.

Other interesting forms of bird and animal life are also found on the Islands of the Moonbird. The black-faced cormorant is found only on these islands, while pelicans, the Australian gannet and the white-crested tern also proliferate. The protected Cape Barren goose, a distinctive grey coloured bird that can weigh up to four kilograms, was once close to extinction, and there is now a ban on killing them. Farmers, however, regard

Above. *Bass Strait's Furneaux Islands contain a vast variety of birdlife such as the Australian gannet.*
Opposite:
Top. *The islands are rocky and windswept.*
Bottom. *These Tasmanian Aborigines, pictured at Oyster Cove, managed to survive exile on Flinders Island in the 1830s. They returned to Tasmania in 1847.*

Vincent Serventy & Associates

Tasmanian Museum and Art Gallery

The Last of The Tasm...
From a photograph taken at Oyster...

them as a menace to their crops and often defy the regulations, taking illegal pot shots at the birds.

The tiger snake, the third most venomous land snake in the world, also lives on the island. Researchers are puzzled as to why the Bass Strait variety is larger and four times more venomous than its mainland counterpart. These differences may be due to the isolation of the islands, and the fact that, except for humans, the snake has little to fear.

The waters of Bass Strait teem with life, and fishing is one of the major occupations of the Furneaux islanders. Scallops and abalone are abundant and the crayfish are Australia's largest and most delicious. These, as well as muttonbird products, are transported from the airport at Whitemark on Flinders Island. Governor King named the island after the explorer Matthew Flinders. It is by far the largest island in the group, being 64 kilometres long and 29 kilometres wide.

The waters of Bass Strait are full of other surprises, some of which have just come to light. The strait is a watery graveyard for some two hundred wrecked ships that have passed the islands' isolated and inhospitable

VINCENT SERVENTY & ASSOCIATES

Right. *Although barren and isolated, the Islands of the Moonbird have a great variety of bird and animal life. The seal population has managed to survive, despite widespread seal hunting.*

Below. *Birds such as the white-fronted tern make the islands a paradise for ornithologists.*

G. MOON/AUSTRALIAN MUSEUM

L. F. SCHICK/AUSTRALIAN MUSEUM

F. DOWLING/AUSTRALIAN MUSEUM

VINCENT SERVENTY & ASSOCIATES

Top left. *The Australian gannet is one of the many birds found on the Islands of the Moonbird.*
Top right. *The large Cape Barren goose was once almost extinct but is now a protected species.*
Above. *Seals and birds are often seen perched on the cliffs of the islands.*

The Islands of the Moonbird are quiet and tranquil with only a thousand inhabitants, mostly farmers and fishermen. The chilly waters of the region contain some 200 shipwrecks and have earned a reputation as Australia's counterpart to the Bermuda Triangle.

shores. Some believe that this is the sea's revenge for human interference with the balance of nature—in farming its waters and decimating the seal population. The *Sydney Cove* sank in 1797 and the wreck was not discovered until 1978. Divers have painstakingly collected and tagged fragments of the ship in the hope that their efforts will reveal a piece of Australia's maritime history. Another casualty of the waters was the barque *G.W. Wolf*, which sank in a gale as recently as 1918. A salvage operation, with the assistance of Royal Australian Air Force helicopters, has been underway. It is not surprising that the area has earned a reputation similar to that of the Bermuda Triangle. These wild seas, which have lured and consumed many a ship, are reluctant to give up their murky secrets.

Treasure of another kind is found on land. The famous Killiecrankie diamond, named after a settlement at Flinders Island, and otherwise known as topaz, is worked by miners such as Allan Wheatley. The clear or white-coloured gemstone from the islands is the best in Australia and among the finest in the world. Some of Allan's pieces of this semiprecious stone weigh as much as one and a half kilograms.

The islanders have witnessed a darker side of Australia's history. In 1830, Wybalenna, on Flinders Island, was reserved for the last of the Tasmanian Aborigines. Removed forcefully from Van Diemen's Land, the forty-four sick and despairing survivors of the race were removed to Oyster Cove (Tasmania) in 1847, where they wasted away from neglect and disease.

Today, the quiet and tranquil Furneaux Islands have a thousand or so inhabitants who farm rich pastures, breed cattle and sheep, or fish for abalone or crayfish, where lawless sealers, pirates and brigands once roamed.

WHALE SAVERS

The practice of whaling has been banned in Australian waters since 1980. Nonetheless, the shoreline may still become a deathtrap for the many varieties of whale that somehow manage to strand themselves.

There have been many incidents of mass whale strandings on Australian beaches: large numbers of tooth (odontocetes) and baleen (mysticetes) whales were beached in Bass Strait in 1911, and on the Tasmanian coast in 1981. These ocean mammals lie stranded, unable to return to the life-giving sea. This behaviour has always been mystifying, and even the experts have long held the theory that the whales are performing an unexplained act of suicide. To some people this seems unlikely, and a new attitude has emerged from whale watchers such as Laurie Levy, 'They're not suicidal;

they get themselves into trouble—they can be rescued.'

An incident in Tasmania in 1981 gave Laurie the opportunity to put his theory into practice. Strahan is a quiet fishing and resort town on Tasmania's rugged west coast and its waters are on the path of the sperm whale (*Physeter catodon*) as it migrates from the Pacific Ocean to the cold Antarctic seas. Set on the shores of beautiful Macquarie Harbour, it is a tranquil part of Tasmania, but for the twenty-seven beached whales it became an inescapable trap.

Above. *The long-finned pilot whale* (Globicephala melaena) *often becomes mystifyingly beached.*
Overleaf. *Long-finned pilot whales lie stranded on the Australian coastline.*

STEVEN FRENCH

STEVEN FRENCH

Above and opposite. *Live mass whale strandings occur throughout the world and are thought to result from navigational errors. The number of animals involved depends on the social habits of the species — those that tend to live in groups, strand in groups.*

ORCA

ORCA

Top and above. *The plight of beached whales in Tasmania and Victoria led to public outcry and shocked the government into action.*
Opposite. *Volunteers use many tactics to keep the whales alive and eventually return the survivors to the ocean.*

After hearing news reports of the strandings, Laurie arrived to give what assistance he could and joined a group of concerned people in attempting to comfort, soothe and hopefully rescue the whales.

Onlookers showed a deep concern for the four-tonne creatures that can reach up to fifteen metres in length, as the volunteers tried unsuccessfully to dig escape channels in the uncooperative sand. Unfortunately, enthusiasm could not replace knowledge, but the experience of wildlife ranger Peter Davis sowed the seeds of a new idea for Laurie. While trying to assist one of the distressed whales, Peter turned its head around, starting the creature on a series of rolls and flips that eventually sent it back into the deep water. Here was a clue to whale rescue that would be tried out some months later.

This time, one hundred and eighty pilot whales (*Globicephala melaena*) were stranded on another Tasmanian beach. Laurie and fellow whale saver Neal Bethune directed a team of volunteers who were joined by enthusiastic beachgoers and bystanders. They pushed and rolled the four-tonne cetaceans into the shallows and then launched them into the ocean. As the whales re-entered their environment they headed out to sea. It took half an hour to launch each whale, and after thirty-six hours of hard work all those still alive were back in the water.

The Tasmanian government was impressed by the great success of the experiment and initiated a whale-saving scheme. Inspired by Laurie and Neal's determination and dedication, Director of Parks and Wildlife Hans Whatstrap exclaimed that 'The main learning experience we have all had here is that what seems impossible may not be impossible.'

The Australian government also took notice and set up a national emergency plan to save stranded whales, while Laurie and Neal established the Whale Rescue Centre in Melbourne. The centre was to be a co-ordination point for future rescue operations, with Neal and Laurie acting in an organisational and advisory capacity. It is gratifying that the authorities are playing their part in what has long been a volunteer-based service. However, there was another difficult test to come.

On a Victorian beach, eighty-seven false killer whales (*Pseudorca crassideus*) became stranded—a common tendency in this species that travels in large schools and is thought to panic in shallow water. Holidaymakers tried to help the creatures, but the Whale Rescue Centre was not informed of the situation. When Laurie heard the news he rushed to the scene, but by the time he arrived a very different solution to the beachings was in operation—the whales were being shot. This unnecessary killing continued until public outcry reached huge proportions. Headlines such as: 'Fury as stranded whales slaughtered', 'Death on the beach', and 'State accused over whale deaths' shocked the government into action and they worked with Neal and Laurie to organise a rescue scheme. Since that time, over two hundred stranded whales have been rescued.

In an interesting example of co-operation between fellow mammals, two young men have disproved a widely held theory of 'suicide strandings', and, in the process, put Australia into the forefront of whale saving.

PYGMY POSSUMS

Australia's marsupials are numerous and indeed some, such as the kangaroo and the koala, have become symbols of the land they inhabit. In addition to the familiar wallaby, bandicoot and wombat, there are many lesser known species that are rarely seen and live quietly among our forests, trees and grasslands.

The mountain pygmy possum (*Burramys parvus*) is one such marsupial; in fact, until as recently as 1966 this little mouse-like animal was considered extinct. Wildlife experts believed that it had become another addition to the list of creatures that have disappeared since the coming of Europeans to Australia. The only mammal that lives exclusively in alpine and sub-alpine regions, the pygmy possum is an unexpected survivor as Ken Shortman and Don Jamieson discovered. Ken and Don found one of these possums in the Mount Hotham region of Victoria. To his astonishment, Ken, although a biologist, could not recognise the species, or find it listed in any of his reference books. As Ken says, 'I thought I was just a very poor zoologist.'

Ken's curiosity about his discovery led him to take the possum to the Fisheries and Wildlife Department, where he hoped an identification would be made. 'When I took it out of its box they said, "My God! What's that," and then they were very excited indeed.' In zoological terms, Ken Shortman's unexpected find was a miracle, and its importance led to the establishment of a team of researchers working exclusively on a newly created pygmy possum project.

Scientists quickly began a thorough search of the Mount Hotham area to estimate numbers of the marsupial, and discovered that the heavily wooded slopes of this mountainous region constituted a vitally important habitat for the estimated two thousand possums. There was, however, one major problem. Despite the fact that the wildlife service fought and won a battle to have Mount Hotham included in a national park, the area includes one of Victoria's most popular ski resorts.

In winter, these high wooded slopes are covered with a blanket of snow, and thousands of eager skiers arrive to enjoy their sport. Skiers mean development: resorts, hotels, ski lifts and roads are needed to cater for the needs of winter sports enthusiasts. Despite the national park status, the number of visitors is increasing each year with corresponding development—wonderful for the skiers, but a disaster for the natural environment and the pygmy possum.

The conservation problem was further complicated by the strangely segregated lifestyle of the possum. The females inhabit the higher slopes, while the males live lower down the mountain. For the species to survive, male and female must meet and breed, and with the

JEAN-PAUL FERRERO/AUSCAPE INTERNATIONAL

Above and opposite. *Until 1966 it was believed that the mountain pygmy possum* (Burramys parvus*) was extinct. A happy discovery in Victoria's highlands has brought to light a great deal of information about this little rock-dwelling creature.*

development of the ski resort coming between them, getting together became increasingly difficult and hazardous. It seemed that the ski industry would thrive at the expense of the rare possum, but, for once, mankind lent a hand to restore the balance of nature.

At the expense of postponing a major development project, a tunnel was constructed under the road to the resort to allow the male possums to make their courtship journeys unhindered and in safety. Now they can travel without risk up the hillside to meet the females and ensure the continuation of their species. The government continues to fund an ongoing study of the little creatures, and, happily, increasingly large numbers of the possums are being seen in the region. The tunnel has been a great success, so much so that the pygmy possum may no longer be rare.

A. SMITH/AUSTRALIAN MUSEUM

Above and opposite. *The mountain pygmy possum is a long-tailed, mouse-like marsupial which inhabits the alpine and subalpine regions of Victoria and New South Wales.*

SECRETS OF SURVIVAL

LEO MEIER/WELDON TRANNIES

On planet Earth, where species evolve, flourish and then sometimes become extinct, insects are the true survivors. Think of the ubiquitous cockroach, or the hordes of flies that pervade an Australian summer, and it is readily obvious that insects have an extraordinary capacity to thrive and survive. It is estimated that there are more than three quarters of a million known species, and probably many more unknown. They are Earth's most adaptable creatures, and the secret of their high survival rate is their amazing ability to adjust to changes in the environment. The leaf insect is a good example. This strange looking creature is hard to observe, having gradually adapted its appearance to blend in with its surroundings so that potential predators are fooled by its resemblance to a leaf.

Insects are voracious and many are considered pests. Some increase their size dramatically within the first six weeks of their short lives, and that often means munching their way through farmers' precious cash crops. Despite our attempts to control them with an arsenal of insecticides and other weapons, the war waged against insects has not been successful. They still survive, and will probably be here long after humans have disappeared from Earth.

Above and opposite. *The insect kingdom contains over three quarters of a million known species, all carefully controlled by nature's accurate and well-planned system. The praying mantis (*Mantis religiosa*) devours other insects as a part of this controlling process.*

WELDON TRANNIES

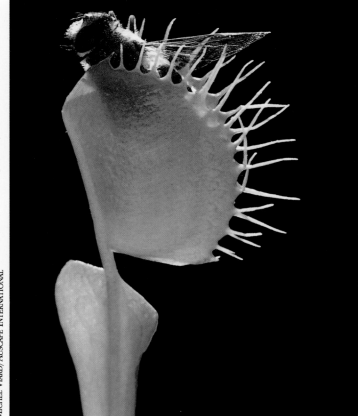

MICHEL VIARD/AUSCAPE INTERNATIONAL

WELDON TRANNIES

Top left. *Termite mounds such as these are found in the north of Australia and can reach 6-7 metres in height.*
Top right. *The carnivorous Venus flytrap* (Dionaea muscipula).
Above. *A hawkmoth caterpillar.*

The strange, gaping-mouthed pitcher plant (Cephalotus follicularis) *which attracts and 'eats' ants.*

Overleaf. *Caterpillars play a vital part in the complex chain of insect control.*
LEO MEIER/WELDON TRANNIES

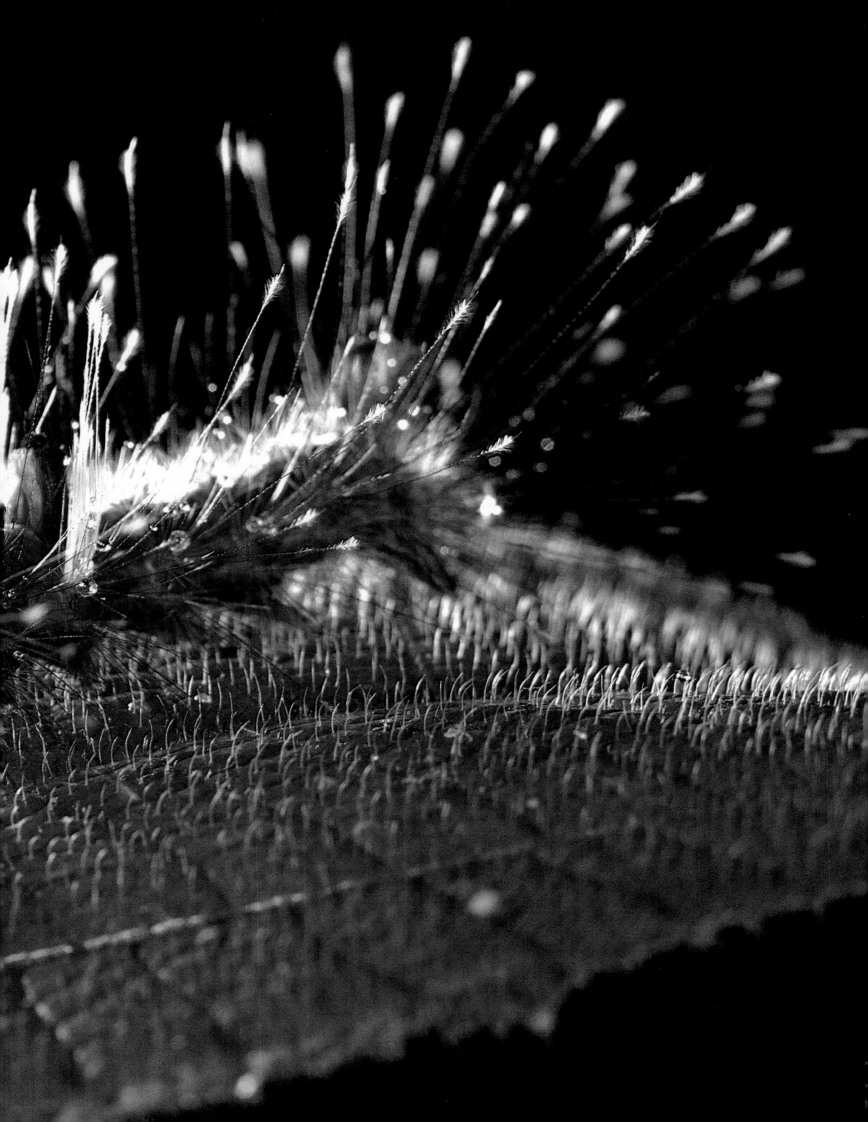

While humans continue to experiment with new methods of pest control, the world of nature has developed its own, more successful, system. With their vast numbers and natural adaptability, insects could easily overrun the world, but the balance of nature has everything under careful control. Birds eat insects, for example; and flies lay eggs on certain caterpillars ensuring their own survival at the expense of an unwilling host that will die in the process. It is all part of the balance of nature that humanity so often destroys.

Plants play their part in controlling insect populations. The fly that decimates the caterpillar is in turn caught by a plant. The Venus flytrap, a native plant of North America, for example, has successfully adapted to Australian conditions, thriving on poor soil and many flies. The oddly shaped Saracenia also traps flies with its gaping 'mouth' that seems to lurk like a carnivorous animal, releasing a chemical to attract its prey. An Australian native carnivore, the tendrilled sundew consumes a wide variety of flying insects. They are attracted to the plant and become trapped by its globules of digestive enzymes. Another introduced plant is the ant-luring pitcher plant, which has made itself at home in northern Australia. The jug-like top of this strange plant attracts ants, then traps them in a mixture of water and enzymes.

Insects also prey on each other. The praying mantis, for example, has a huge appetite for other insects, while ants eat certain larvae. Nature works so well until humans interfere with this carefully created balance.

Crops such as cotton provide vast feeding and breeding grounds for insects. Thus, insecticides have been developed to protect cotton and other kinds of crops. The controversial insecticide DDT was once the farmer's greatest weapon, but scientists have found that insects gradually become resistant to it. In the case of the cotton bollworm, DDT applications were strengthened several times but it was found that this only developed stronger resistance in the insect pest. A new product was tested — pyrethrum, a natural substance from a daisy, which was later produced synthetically. A so-called 'soft' insecticide, it did have the advantage of having little effect on the environment but, by 1985, farmers were misusing the product and the bollworm had become resistant to this also.

Research scientists now provide a computer service to help farmers control cotton insect pests, advising which insecticides to use and when. But in the case of cotton, the problem will not go away. The more chemical insecticides are used, the more nature's

*The sundew (*Drosera auriculata*), an Australian native, is another plant which helps to control the numbers of the insect kingdom. It attracts flies and other insects, which become hopelessly trapped by the plant's sticky enzymes.*

Leo Meier/Weldon Trannies

*Insects are the earth's most adaptable creatures.
They have survived most of humankind's
attempts to control them.
Above. A leaf-like mantid.
Right. A tropical species of fly.
Opposite. Green tree ants.*

balance tips towards destruction. Most people are aware that termites are a pest: they eat through many types of timber, even houses. But nature provides them with the very important role of enriching the soil. An indiscriminate use of insecticides may eradicate the termite, which would have a severe effect on Australia's grazing lands.

Birds such as the Willy wagtail are another vital link in nature's chain of control. Their growing chicks need constant feeding, and insects are one of their favourite and indeed vital foods. If insecticides are used indiscriminately, the insects will disappear and so will the birds.

Humankind has a duty to redress this imbalance. Though not an easy task, at least there is a new awareness of the fragility of the ecology, and scientists are striving to protect the many varieties of insect with their importance to most aspects of life on Earth.

Leo Meier/Weldon Trannies

FAIRY PENGUINS

J. R. NAPIER/AUSTRALIAN MUSEUM

Above and opposite. *Like many rare Australian species, the tiny fairy penguin (*Eudyptula minor*) is in danger of extinction.*

David Barton is an unusual man. At first sight this muscled, tattooed trawler skipper looks like the last person to have an affection and concern for birdlife, but appearances can be deceptive. The man who has been in his time a top grade rugby player, police officer, soldier and long distance truckie is now called 'tweetie pie', but only from a safe distance, by his disbelieving mates.

David loves birds, and none more than Australia's famous pint-sized fairy penguin (*Eudyptula minor*), which inhabits the southern shorelines. There used to be thousands of these birds but now, apart from the penguins in sanctuaries such as Phillip Island, the population has diminished. A colony of fairy penguins at Eden, in southern New South Wales, has been dramatically declining in recent years, and it was this struggling little group that David Barton became determined to help. David believes that the birds owe

their survival to the fact that their nests are protected by an overhanging cliff. The penguin has few real enemies, but their most dangerous enemy is mankind. Tourism and development disturb the birds' habitat and make it difficult for the growing penguins to find nest sites. Dogs are also a problem. As David explains, 'The penguins have been wandering over the top of the cliff into people's backyards, and that way they're getting into trouble with the dogs.'

Time was running out for the penguins at Eden before David arrived. The trawler skipper has spent several years fighting single-handed to save his favourite birds. He tags them and records their breeding patterns, and generally shows a father's concern for the helpless chicks and their welfare. Although David is an amateur, he has impressed the ornithological world with his knowledge, photographs and writing. He has become quite an expert on the fairy penguin.

John Krutop/The Age

Above. *David Barton, the trawler skipper who became an unlikely champion of the penguins' cause.*
Left. *Fairy penguins take their evening walk along the shore.*

So what initially inspired this tough man of the sea to take up the penguins' cause? When he was a boy he used to steal birds' eggs, but an incident when he was twelve years old changed his behaviour. He was out sailing his yacht when it overturned and he had to swim for the shore. Barely surviving the experience, he changed his opinions about a lot of things. 'I'd had it you know,' he recalls. 'I was sinking and just about unconscious, and I distinctly remember making a deal with God . . . something along the lines of—you get me out of this, and I'll leave the birds' eggs alone.' It was the beginning of a lifelong interest in the creatures whose nests he had been robbing.

Whatever the source of his inspiration, David has done much to protect the penguins' fragile existence, and the numbers of the small colony have slowly increased. Their hold on their environment is still precarious though, and now they do not have David Barton to watch over them—David's fishing catch diminished dramatically and he had to sell up and move away from the area. Thankfully, the people of Eden have been inspired by David's concern and have taken up his cause to help save the unique fairy penguins who still perform their waddling nightly parade along the shore, and who cling tenaciously to their last outpost.

UNDERWATER COMMUNITIES

I. R. MARRINER/WELDON TRANNIES

Australia's strange and beautiful underwater world is alive with colour, shape and movement.

Opposite and overleaf. *There are many varieties of anemone, belonging to the group Coelenterata. These soft bodied animals catch their prey by stinging it with their tentacles and folding it into their mouths.*
REG MORRISON/WELDON TRANNIES

Beneath the surface of the sea lies a rich and beautiful world—a world which most of us unfortunately will never see or explore. An amazing variety of interesting and sometimes bizarre and surprising creatures live there.

Barnacles, with which most of us are familiar, are those crusty looking objects that cling to the surface of boats or jetties. But underneath the sea there is a far more attractive variety, characterised by feathery, tendril-like, jointed arms that wave about, sifting food particles through the water.

Coral is another organism that has to wait for its food. The house-bound coral feeds almost accidentally; it lies in wait for drifting plankton to come its way. Yet coral colonies thrive on this strange feeding process—the huge expanse of the Great Barrier Reef is evidence of this.

Unlike coral, the flower-like sea anemones have the advantage of movement, albeit at a snail's pace. They do not range far, being creatures that are basically bundles of jelly that flex as they open and close.

One of the ocean's prettiest creatures has an inappropriate and unpleasant name—the batwing sea slug. This delicate, purple-coloured sea animal grazes on the seabed, but, unlike those species already described, it is able to move about easily. It is able to flap its butterfly-like wings and 'fly' through the water.

The spiky decorator crab is one of the strangest sea creatures. It has obtained its name from the bizarre lengths it goes to in 'decorating' and disguising itself. Many underwater species have the ability to alter their form, but none go to the lengths of this crab, which spends most of its life preening and posing, as though it were vainly dressing itself in front of a mirror. Every part of the shell is covered with all the finery its reef environment can offer: weed, coral and even small rocks are used to create a strange and jumbled fancy dress, worthy of a carnival parade. The finery adheres to the shell due to the presence of a strong waterproof glue, released from the crab's salivary glands. From time to time the decorator crab changes shells and then has to create a new costume all over again. It is a fascinating, if little understood, form of underwater behaviour.

These creatures are just a few of the fascinating varieties which make up Australia's marine life. The world under the water is completely different to the world above and it is perhaps surprising to find that there is as much variety and complexity here as on land.

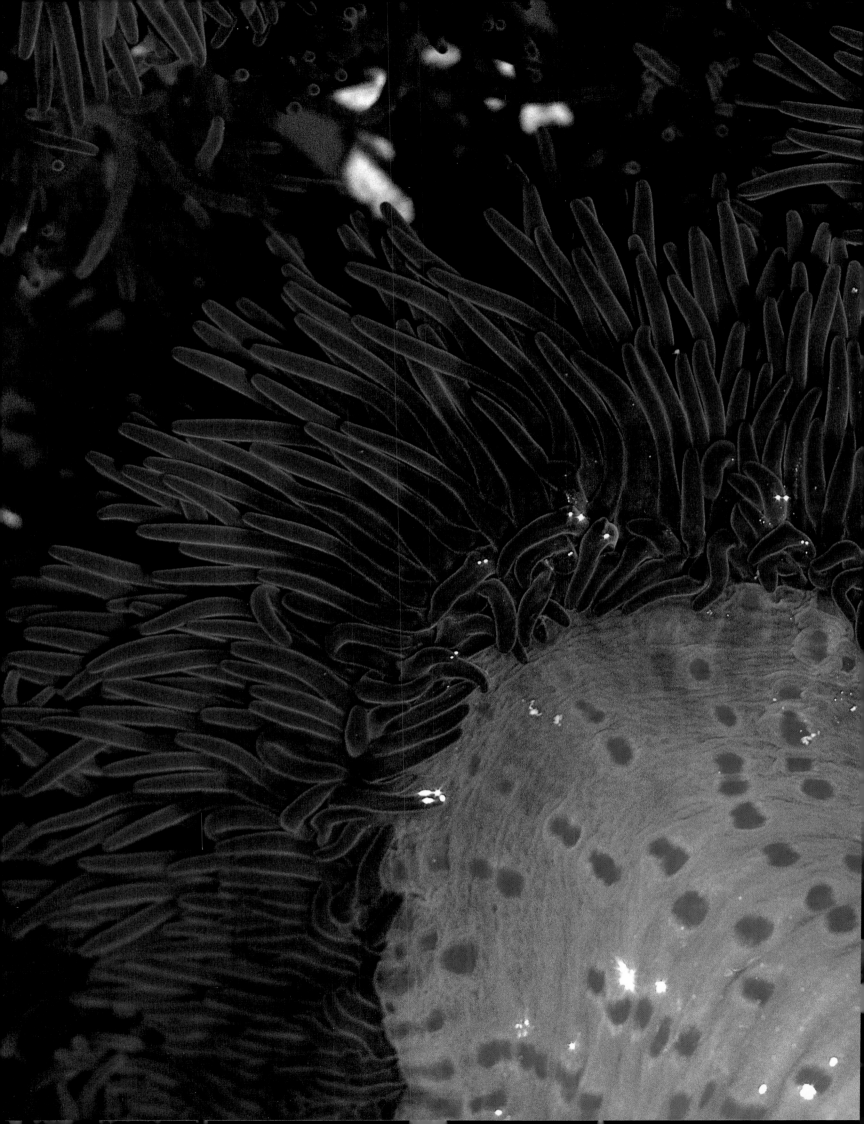

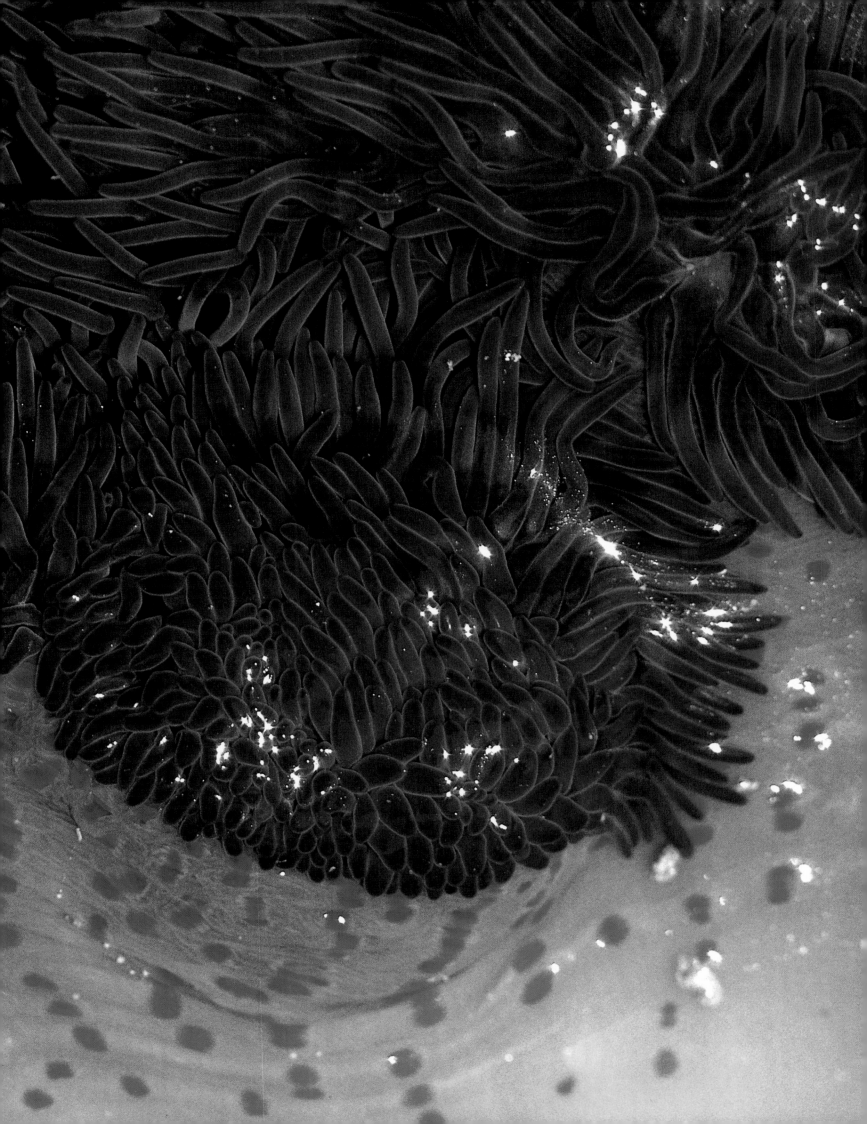

Top and above. *The Great Barrier Reef is one of the world's most intriguing natural wonders. Complex symbiotic relationships have developed between many of its plants and animals: the tiny anemone fish lives amongst and is protected by the tentacles of the anemone, which offer it security but are lethal to other creatures.*

The octopus, seen here devouring a shellfish, is a surprisingly intelligent creature. Scientists have discovered that these multi-limbed marine animals can even open a twist-top jar to reach their food.

BEN CROPP/AUSCAPE INTERNATIONAL

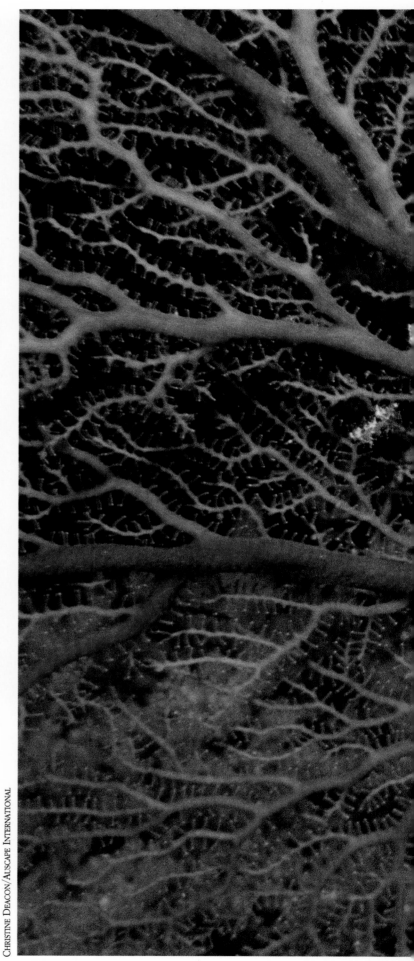

CHRISTINE DEACON/AUSCAPE INTERNATIONAL

Above *This colourful underwater coral garden is host to a vast marine community, unsurpassed in diversity by any other ecosystem. In contradiction to its name, the Great Barrier Reef is not a single barrier but is made up of a variety of islands, cays and reefs, stretching for 1,250 nautical miles along the coast of Queensland. The colours and textures of its many species of coral, fishes and other sea creatures have been the inspiration for many an artist and designer.*

Right. *The sea anemone is a 'bundle of jelly' that has the ability to move, albeit very slowly.*

Overleaf. *The decorator crab adorns itself with a strange and jumbled fancy dress — weed, coral, small rocks and anything else the reef has to offer. This bizarre decoration actually serves as a very effective camouflage.*

KEVIN DEACON/AUSCAPE INTERNATIONAL

NUMBATS

The geographic isolation of the Australian continent has produced a fascinating diversity of creatures—birds, insects, reptiles and mammals—but none is as interesting as the unique collection of marsupials. These mammals produce their young only partly developed, and then carry them in the safety of a body pouch.

Some of these Australian marsupials are endangered —including the exclusive numbat (*Myrmecobius fasciatus*), whose home is confined to a small part of southwest Western Australia. Indeed, this tiny creature, just 25 centimetres long, has become the State's animal emblem. However, it is rarely seen. A walk through the eucalypt forests of the region is more likely to produce an encounter with other creatures: the echidna, shingle back lizard, or perhaps a carpet snake. The most likely place to spot a numbat would be in the hollows of a fallen eucalypt log where the numbat's favourite food, the termite, is found.

The numbat lives alone, wandering over its marked territory of about half a hectare. It is an appealing creature: small, reddish brown in colour with a black and white banded rump and a long bushy tail. The small eyes see little and the pointed ears are not very effective either, but the numbat survives on its vital supply of termites, thanks to its heightened sense of smell. Numbats were first noted by European settlers in 1836, and were misleadingly named banded anteaters. They are indeed striped, but termites, not ants appeal to this marsupial.

A. G. WELLS/AUSTRALIAN MUSEUM

The numbat (Myrmecobius fasciatus) is one of the smallest of Australia's marsupials.
Confined to southwestern Western Australia, it is so exclusive to this area that it has become the State's emblem.
With its highly developed sense of smell and long pink tongue, the numbat is perfectly adapted for consumption of termites.

Opposite. The adult numbat is just 25 centimetres long and produces young weighing less than a gram.
Overleaf. The numbat's distinctive black and white bands on reddish brown fur blend in well with its woodland environment.
JIRI LOCHMAN/AUSTRALIAN MUSEUM

C. A. HENLEY/AUSCAPE INTERNATIONAL

The new born, embryo-like numbat is minute—the size of a grain of wheat and weighing less than one gram. It is amazing that the young survive this early stage, but the mother suckles them for four months. During the first few weeks they begin to grow a little hair and develop the beginnings of ears and tiny hind legs. By five months they are still being suckled, but begin to learn to chew solid food. Using X-ray film, the secrets of the adult numbat's eating methods have been revealed. The numbat does not chew, but simply flicks at the termites with its long pink tongue. This tongue is disproportionately long, being half its entire body length. An adult of the species also has fifty-two teeth— more than any other marsupial, and more than most land mammals. This is one of the mysteries of this rare creature.

Overall, the nursing period lasts for six months, a long time compared with other marsupials. The babies stay close to their mother, even clinging to her back, but eventually they fend for themselves, and within the first year they, too, breed.

The future, however, looks bleak for the survival of one of the world's rarest creatures. Numbats are not easily bred in captivity, and their numbers are decreasing in the wild. Although termites, their major food source, are usually plentiful, bushfires threaten both the numbat and its prey. In addition, land clearing removes and destroys the vital fallen trees—the termites's life support system. As so often happens in nature, human interference upsets a delicate and well-balanced ecology. The little seen numbat of Western Australia may become even more elusive and, if we are not careful, extinct.

Left and above. *Records of the numbat date back to 1836, but as its numbers have declined it has become an increasingly rare sight in Western Australian woodlands.*

ADVENTURE

Adventure has always played an important role in the life of Australians. These mountain riders help to keep the tradition alive.

COLIN BEARD/WELDON TRANNIES

CHALLENGE OF LAKE EYRE

AUSTRALIAN BROADCASTING CORPORATION

Many people have been fascinated by Lake Eyre, including Donald Campbell who hurtled across the gleaming saltpan of the lake in the Proteus *Bluebird II* to establish the first world land speed record set in Australia. John and Roma Dulhunty chose a somewhat slower form of transport but one which better served their purpose. Their light but strong galvanised water tank, mounted lengthwise on the back of a utility truck was the most practical mobile home for their lifestyle and work amid conditions that would severely test the mental and physical resources of most people.

For the Dulhuntys, Lake Eyre was a challenge. Although John and Roma were both over seventy years old, they were not ready to take up a pipe, slippers and knitting. John, a retired geologist, and Roma, his field assistant, believed there was still work to be done and challenges to be faced.

Lake Eyre is certainly isolated. A dry salt bed of approximately 5,800 square kilometres lies beside the Simpson Desert in central South Australia. There are 2,000 kilometres between Dulhuntys' comfortable home in a leafy harbourside suburb of Sydney and Lake Eyre.

John and Roma headed for Lake Eyre, in their wrinkled-metal gypsy-like caravan which pitched and tossed like a strange vessel in a sea of sand, stone and spinifex. One of the objects of their planned research was to test John's theory that Lake Eyre, estimated to be 12 metres below sea level, was still sinking.

No one had ever reported seeing so much water in the lake as there was after the deluge of 1974. John calculated that it was the deepest flooding in five hundred years. After the deluge, what had been sand, mud and salt looked like the great inland sea that so many early explorers had sought in vain. Four years later, Lake Eyre had returned to ankle-deep slush, its watery expanse sucked up greedily by the dry desert.

Despite the risk of stepping into a patch of treacherous quicksand, four metres deep in some places, John and Roma plunged enthusiastically into their task of collecting evidence. According to John, there was not 'any time when we thought we should give it up — that it was too hard.' And as Roma added, 'We have a lot of tricks up our sleeves when it comes to this type of environment and we feel confident that we could get out — unless we had some very bad luck.'

Above. *Ageless adventurers Roma and John Dulhunty.*
Opposite. *Lake Eyre's dry salt beds stretch over a vast 10,000 square-kilometre area.*

Overleaf. *During their many trips to Lake Eyre, the Dulhuntys saw much of this arid claypan scenery.*
REG MORRISON/WELDON TRANNIES

To aid them in their work, they went armed with a modern weapon against the oozy lake — a lightweight hovercraft. 'It was certainly a wild and woolly animal!' gasped John with a modicum of relief and a lot of admiration after a skittish test run. 'It has a mind of its own, but it was really useful on the lake.'

On their first trip, the Dulhuntys camped by the lake for sixty days, surveying by day and writing up their notes by night. From a small window in the back door of their water-tank home, their gentle debate over finer points on their findings drifted into the starry stillness in which their voices were the only sounds.

The couple returned to the great lake every year for twelve years. During those twelve years, John and Roma used all kinds of transport — the hovercraft, a four-wheel drive vehicle and Honda tricycles to explore the inhospitable surroundings of Lake Eyre. They explored the north shore to the Warburton Estuary, and later, they were the first white Australians to cross the treacherous

mud from the eastern side, and also the estuary of Cooper's Creek. According to Roma, they 'found fossilised remains of extinct marsupials from 30,000 years ago, indicating that the climate was certainly much wetter then.' At the northern end of the lake, they found eroded sandhills built by sand and dust blown out of the lake to form the Simpson Desert about 10,000 years ago.

John and Roma have wonderful memories of their years spent at Lake Eyre. As Roma reminisces, 'The lake has given us more reward, excitement, adventure and challenge than we have ever had in our lives.' Only John's heart condition could put an end to the arduous trekking. Now Lake Eyre is just a dry, glistening temptation 2,000 kilometres away. Roma has written three books on Lake Eyre and they both enjoy their view of all the activity on Sydney Harbour. That trusty old water-tank truck is still in the back yard. 'We could never let it go. It is still used for short trips,' say the ageless adventurers.

AUSTRALIAN BROADCASTING CORPORATION

John and Roma's unusual water tank mounted on a utility truck served as a 'home' during their twelve Lake Eyre expeditions.

SHARK CATCHERS

The fearsome tiger shark (Galeocerdo cuvier) *in search of prey.*
Overleaf. *A tiger shark feeds on an unfortunate marlin.*
BEN CROPP/AUSCAPE INTERNATIONAL

There are many ways of making a living, but Ian Croll's choice is unusual. Ian spends much of his time in close association with one of nature's most feared and infamous creatures — the shark. He hunts the sharks not to destroy them but to give them a new home in his marine garden on beautiful Magnetic Island, off Townsville on the north Queensland coast.

It is not, however, just sharks that Ian is interested in. He needs all kinds of fish to stock his aquarium. Magnetic Island is a popular tropical holiday resort that receives almost 60,000 tourists each year. Most of them visit Ian's aquarium where more than thirty sharks are the big attraction, especially at feeding time. Spectators watch with cautious fascination as Ian feeds fish to his 'friends' while at the same time giving a running commentary. He explains that although there are smaller fish mingling with the sharks, they are quite safe unless they become sick or show signs of weakness.

Ian has had many years of experience in learning the tricks of handling these fearsome predators of the deep and has had some of his sharks for ten years. But he still would not trust them. He says that sharks cannot be tamed; they act purely on instinct, and the urge to feed is a particularly strong one. Ian has several painful reminders of this, although the closest they have come to nibbling him is when they took a small piece of a finger along with the fish he dangles into the tank. He says you have to concentrate: If it fastens on to the rest of your hand, you could have a problem.'

Ian finds his sharks in the clear blue waters of the Great Barrier Reef, and is always on the lookout for bigger and better specimens to improve his collection. Catching them with a hook and a strong line can cause fatal injuries to the sharks, so Ian enlists the help of friends to devise a plan of action. He uses a large nylon net to catch the sharks, and, with one man on board the boat and three in the water, they are able to net some decent-sized specimens. Ian looks for reef whaler sharks of around two metres in length. If the sharks are small Ian throws them back and keeps looking.

In all of his shark-catching days, Ian has had only one close brush with death, something he will never be able to forget. While he was spearing a fish a shark approached from out of nowhere. The shark paused for what seemed one heart-stopping moment, then swam away. But it came back for a second look at its potential meal. As Ian recalls, 'I thought that I was going to die. The shark turned and he lined me up and came at me at an extraordinary speed but then he swam away and disappeared. To this day I can see it in slow motion exactly as it happened at that time.'

That was close enough for Ian, but it still did not deter him from pursuing his underwater activities. Now, with a net, he and his friends suspend a bait and wait for a shark to appear. When a large one obligingly swims into the waiting trap and struggles to find its way out of the mesh that encircles it, the shark catchers haul the writhing creature on board their boat. Once on board, Ian Croll returns the net to the water, continuing his risky task of bringing these feared killers back alive.

Even though Ian Croll 'plays' with the sharks, he has a healthy respect for their untamed nature.

QUIET CHALLENGE

It is hard to describe the thrill of soaring on thermal air currents, flying free and gazing down at the patchwork ground below. With no mechanical equipment to hinder a face-to-face confrontation of humankind with the elements, gliding is a very personal and intense experience. It is also a sport that requires skill, concentration and a deep understanding of the natural forces that form the glider's power source — currents of land-heated, rising air.

Despite Australia's long and impressive history of flying, with its pioneers such as Sir Charles Kingsford Smith and the early outback Queensland QANTAS pilots, gliding has never featured strongly in Australia's list of aerial successes. Internationally, Australia's reputation in gliding circles has always been, to say the least, modest.

That was before Bill Riley. Bill had retired from a successful business career and was living on the Gold Coast of Queensland. He had been flying gliders as a hobby since boyhood and was hooked on the sport. In his determination to put Australia on the world gliding map, he decided to establish a school in southern New South Wales, and make his hobby a full-time occupation. Bill's theory was that if you have the best school, you will ultimately produce the best glider pilots.

To help in this ambitious task, Bill Riley recruited two unusual and dedicated men. Ingo Renner is originally from Germany, and was Bill's only instructor

Above. *Australian gliding was well below world class standards until Bill Riley established his school in southern New South Wales. Novices and experienced glider pilots flock to Bill's school to improve their skills, and benefit from excellent instruction and equipment.*

when the school first started in 1970. Bert Persson, Bill's other recruit, is an engineer and an aerobatics expert. Both Ingo and Bert have the attributes of single-mindedness and ability, and when Bill recruited these two men, both had a history of active involvement in gliding clubs, both were gliding instructors and both had completed many long distance flights. Flights over distances of 500 kilometres are not unusual but require a lot of skill and concentration. Studying the air patterns and using the glider to its maximum ability requires, as Bill says, 'complete and utter concentration while you are actually doing the task.'

Since the commencement of the school, Ingo has won the Australian Gliding Championships on many occasions and has been chosen to represent Australia in the World Gliding Championships on every occasion since 1972, when he was placed sixth (the highest placing ever achieved by an Australian). He was placed second in 1974 at Waikerie in Australia, first in Finland in 1976 and won the championship on three more occasions, in the United States, Italy and Australia, thereby becoming the only pilot to win the World Gliding Championships four times. Ingo has also won the Smirnoff Derby, a glider race across the United States, and the Hitachi Masters gliding contest.

The school has flourished. Set in the open country, amid the clear skies and reliable weather of southern New South Wales, it has the obvious advantage of location, but, without the efforts of Bill, Ingo and Bert, it would not have achieved such success. Many novices come to learn, but the school also attracts experienced pilots from Australia as well as the United States, Europe and Japan who come to improve their flying techniques and benefit from the wealth of experience that these instructors have to offer. The excellent reputation of Bill Riley's school has helped to create more interest in the sport, more qualified instructors and a much more respectable status for Australian gliding.

Meanwhile, the three men enjoy their chosen sport, and often take to the skies together in friendly contest. It keeps their competitive edge sharp, and allows them to indulge in their passion. The streamlined craft wing over pastures like three long-armed crucifixes; flying straight, then flipping in a show of aerobatic gymnastics. It is quiet and peaceful up there as they flow with the elements, although as Bill points out, 'You worry about the quietness alright, because if it goes absolutely quiet, the glider is not flying — it has stalled.'

It is a thrill nevertheless, and a sensation that is difficult to put into words. Ingo Renner says that only a poet could describe the thrill that glider pilots feel.

The quiet thrill of gliding. Up there above the trees, the streamlined glider soars, falls, twists and turns in tune with the air currents. It's a difficult art that takes a great deal of skill and concentration, but it is also a sensation that glider pilots become addicted to.

LEO MEIER/WELDON TRANNIES

THREE MEN IN A RAFT

RAY JOYCE/WELDON TRANNIES

They called themselves 'Australia's most incompetent explorers', and a first look at this unlikely trio certainly would not have warranted the use of the normal adventurous adjectives like 'intrepid', 'brave' or 'fearless'. John Hepworth was 60 years old, grey, bearded and had only one lung; John Hindle was over 120 kilograms in weight and looked a likely candidate for a 'Life. Be in it!' campaign warning against the dangers of inactivity; and Patrick Amer was a British army transport officer who couldn't drive. Together they set out to make the longest raft journey in Australia's history. None of them were young, they were all city dwellers, and eccentric with an eccentric story to tell. On the unstable looking sheet metal and polystyrene raft called *George*, skippered by Alan Shinnick, they set out on the long journey. *George* was the team's lifeline for forty-eight days.

This improbable group took on the many moods of the mighty River Murray: from the highlands of New South Wales, along the New South Wales/Victorian border, through to South Australia, to the point where the river spills into Lake Alexandrina and, finally, the ocean. It was a journey of over 2,400 kilometres along the continent's longest river and none of the men had

any real idea of what they would encounter in the next seven weeks. Skipper Alan had some knowledge of the lower reaches of the river, but the others were untried for such a demanding adventure. *George* was a bit of a gamble too — the raft was completed just two days before the team set off.

The big day arrived and the three men, the skipper, and *George*, launched into their adventure. Almost as soon as they were farewelled by friends and well-wishers, they learned that the upper reaches of the Murray are full of hazards. The waters there are freezing and fast-flowing, and the path of the raft was often blocked by trees, snags and other obstructions. It was not long before the adventurers ran into trouble when willow trees blocked their route. They became entangled and had a difficult struggle to free their craft. After just one day, *George* was a mess.

Above. *Tranquil Lake Hume.*
Opposite. *From the highlands to the sea: the adventurers travelled over 2,400 kilometres along the River Murray.*
Overleaf. *The river snakes its way through Victorian woodlands.*
LEO MEIER/WELDON TRANNIES

Rounding a Murray bend.

Patrick at the helm.

Australia's most adventurous explorers.

George — the makeshift but trusty raft.

John Hepworth on camera.

Onlookers greet the team at Horseshoe Bend wharf.

BRIAN GRAVES

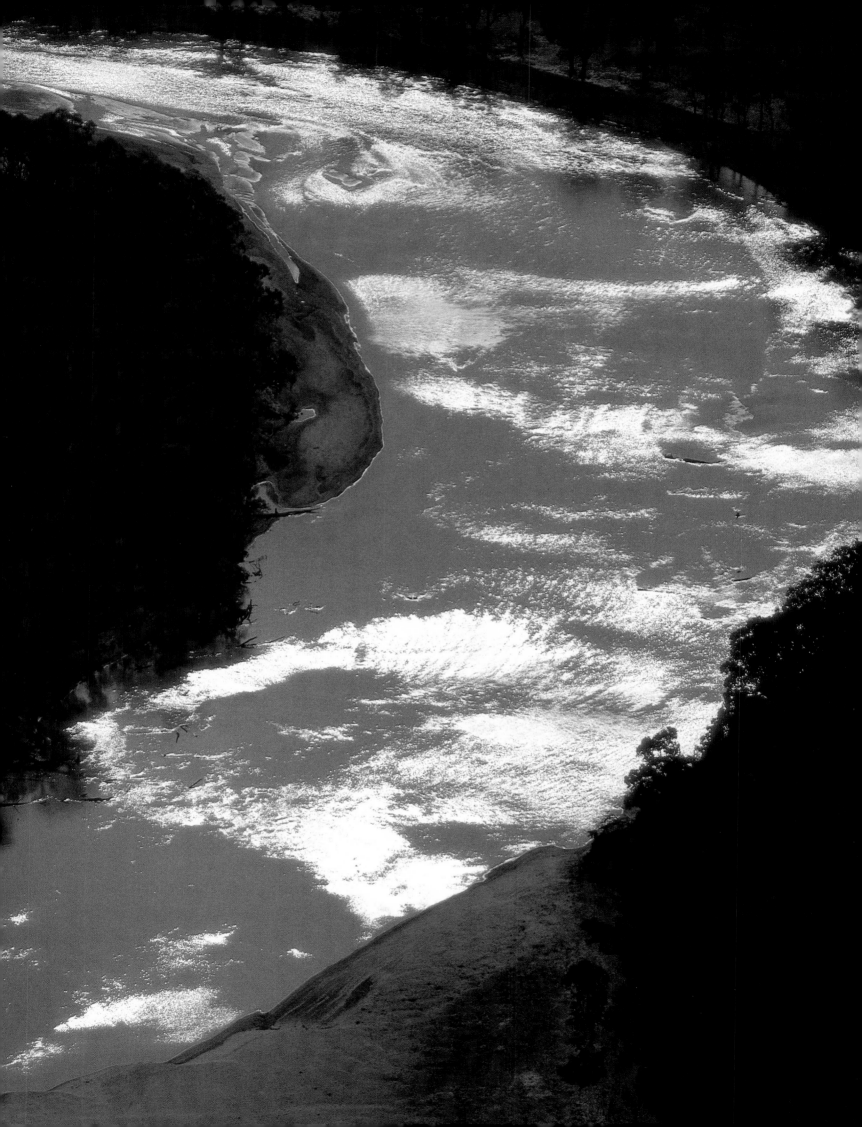

However, Lake Hume, near Albury, was reached without much further incident, and Hindle and Hepworth began work on their proposed book about the adventure. They bashed away on the old typewriters while *George* was propelled across Lake Hume. The lake was formed in 1934 when a newly constructed dam flooded these southern New South Wales pastures. It was here that the men discovered the raft was taking in water — it was holed during the collision with the willow trees. This was to be the first of many troubles.

Further downstream, they reached the second man-made lake — Lake Mulwala. It is a desolate place without wildlife and with only the stumps of rotting dead trees protruding from the water. The only signs of life are the herds of Murray Grey cattle that browse along the river banks. Further on, the scenery changed to include huge stands of red gums, and the men occasionally caught glimpses of kangaroos and emus.

The delicately balanced ecology of this region is threatened by the proposal to build another dam, and the local farmers' need for irrigation water. Since the dams were built, the land surrounding the river floods in summer, preventing young seedlings from taking root, and conservationists are concerned that the magnificent forests will gradually die. Sadly, the value of the Murray River as a natural resource is not recognised. Its ecology faces great dangers unless far-sighted measures are taken to redress the current imbalance of nature.

By the time the adventurers neared Echuca, they had spent seventeen days on the river. New hazards loomed on the water, river temperatures were cold and they were concerned about the risk of collision with paddle steamers. These remnants of a once thriving and vital transport industry still travel the river, but only upstream as far as Echuca, where the navigational limit is marked by undredged waters and a sharp narrowing of the river. This region receives little rainfall, but irrigation has made the land fertile and farming has boomed. Ironically, this farmland is slowly becoming a desert, due to too much, rather than too little water. As more land is cleared and drenched with irrigation water, underlying mineral salts are brought to the surface, killing off vegetation and causing grave concern to the farming industry.

As the team approached Mildura, a storm hit, causing chaos aboard the flimsy raft. By morning, however, all was calm and without further incident, the men reached the infamous Devil's Elbow — a sharp bend in the river which has long been a hazard to paddle steamers. Surprisingly, after weeks on their tiny raft, the novice adventurers were still full of cheer and enthusiasm for the project. But the biggest challenge was yet to come.

In forty-eight days on the river, the explorers saw the many moods of the Murray. Near Mildura (left) and at nearby Merbein (above).

RAY JOYCE/WELDON TRANNIES

As the Murray enters South Australia, its mood changes yet again. The river widens and is flanked by 40 metre high clay cliffs. This is the citrus, grape and soft fruit growing region known as the Riverland.

The four men were well into South Australia now and although the trip was nearing its end, they were worried by the daunting reputation of the choppy Lake Alexandrina crossing. *George* survived the rigours of the river, but was worn and leaking badly. For the men, it was vital that their craft reached the journey's end, which was on the ocean side of the lake. Dissension threatened the cameraderie that had pervaded the long voyage.

John Hindle believed it was time to call it a day: 'I just want to get out of this thing without really getting too wet . . . this thing is split. The whole damn thing is going to break up into four pieces.' Patrick also thought that reason should prevail over John Hepworth's perhaps misplaced dedication to completing the course they had set themselves: 'You are injecting a false sense of enthusiasm into this venture that I don't care for.' Hepworth remained adamant though — they were going to continue across the lake to the sea. So the reluctant heroes pressed on to finish their journey.

They never really completed the journey, for once they were on Lake Alexandrina waves swamped the tired craft. Helpless and in danger of sinking, a local fisherman took them in tow, while a South Australian patrol boat stood by to offer assistance. And so the unlikely adventurers' journey ended, just eight kilometres short of their target — the southern ocean.

Two thousand, four hundred kilometres and forty-eight days after their naively optimistic launching, high up in the Great Dividing Range, the adventurers proved that adventure is not only for the young and fit, but that endurance is all a state of mind. It was indeed a remarkable journey. John Hepworth said it all as they made their final landfall: 'I declare this voyage well and truly done.'

BACKYARD WINGS

Flying was mainly the sport of the rich, that is, before the days of ultra lights. These light aircraft revolutionised aviation for they have brought the sport within the reach of anyone with limited finance, with creative ability and with a sense of adventure. Not surprisingly, ultra light flying has many followers and aspiring aviators all over Australia are turning to the sport.

Hang-gliding paved the way for the development of ultra lights. A logical extension of the free flying glider was the addition of a motor and wheels to create an aircraft that was easy to assemble, cheap to run and relatively simple to fly.

The dream of a flying machine that was within everyone's budget led enthusiasts such as Hans Litjens to undertake some dangerous and unpredictable experiments. The earliest designs were bulky and difficult to manoeuvre and looked like heavyweights in comparison with the small, compact machines of today. Hans remembers his early take-off attempts, which he says were 'very difficult, particularly without wheels, because you have to hold the right angle of a tack. You have to hold the whole thing up in the air and then, when you open the throttle, the thrust, you have to run whether you like it or not.'

Due to difficulties with these running take-offs, wheels were added to the machines. Hans recalls that 'Every take-off was . . . very dangerous, so the only way to go was to put wheels on them.'

Landings were just as difficult as the take-offs. Once the aircraft was successfully airborne, it was another matter to return it safely to earth. Bumpy and dangerous landings were common, but enthusiasts such as Hans persisted in their efforts and perfected the technique. It was the beginning of the flying revolution.

As the sport gained popularity, the Department of Aviation issued a ruling which stated that ultra lights should not fly over the height of 500 feet (155 metres), or in controlled airspace, at night, in cloud or over cities and towns. Despite these limitations, there was still plenty of Australian airspace to explore, and the ranks of the backyard wings brigade swelled rapidly. In sheds and garages throughout the country, amateurs assembled from wood, plastic, wire and aluminium their enormous variety of flimsy craft. They reached for the sky in search of the thrill of flying.

Ultra light flying is not a sport only for amateurs. Even commercial airline pilots such as Rod Birrel became enthused by this new form of flying. The sport appealed to Rod because the ultra light pilot is able to control his machine totally. He believes that this is 'real flying', and that 'the controls and systems on a jet are quite different to an ultra light. In modern jets, controls are automated. In an ultra light, the major difference from a jet is that the pilot does everything directly. He moves a stick which moves the control by a cable or a tail shaft and there is no other interference with the machine. This means that ultra lights fly much more quickly and instantaneously than, say, a jet would.'

As ultra lights have come out of the backyard workshops and taken to the air, there have been many modifications in the design. The machine that was one step up from a hang-glider now comes in an amazing variety of shapes and sizes. Many ultra lights still look primitive and flimsy, with the pilot sitting exposed and vulnerable under the wings; and bumpy landings are still a common hazard of the sport. Some machines are reminiscent of the bizarre contraptions from the era of *Those Magnificent Men in Their Flying Machines*, but

*Hans Litjens' early ultra light flying experiments involved some hair-raising take-offs and landings in machines without wheels (*left*) and later with wheels (*right*).*

ACTION GRAPHICS

Above and overleaf. *Modern ultra lights have come a long way. Monoplanes like these are graceful,
scaled-down versions of more conventional light aircraft.*

with new varieties of craft becoming airborne, the small home-built monoplanes are capable of performing the most extraordinary aerobatic feats, similar to those of a more conventional light aircraft. The sport is definitely growing bigger and more sophisticated.

With interest in ultra lights growing, there is a concern that safety standards should be set and maintained. It is a potentially dangerous sport. Out of his concern for safety in ultra light flying, Noel Cruise, a former RAAF jet fighter pilot, has initiated an ultra light flying course which he believes is essential. As he says, 'They are very much like real aeroplanes in every sense of the word. You can fly them like real aeroplanes. You can crash them like real aeroplanes. So even though you do not require a formal licence, you do need to know how to fly, or be shown how to fly, the aeroplane.' Noel

compares it to a child riding a trail bike. The youngster may not need a licence to ride it, but the parents would be irresponsible if they did not teach the child to ride the bike properly. Noel says that 'It is the same sort of thing.'

Various safety devices such as an emergency parachute rescue attachment have been developed and are being experimented with to ensure the safety of the ultra light pilots. It is important for the future of the sport that ultra light flying maintains a good reputation for safety.

For the daring, however, there is no sensation like it. Flying over the Victorian coast's Twelve Apostles, or skimming low across the Australian countryside in their open ultra lights, is an experience that none of the growing band of backyard wings pilots would be without.

SNOWY MOUNTAIN RIDERS

COLIN BEARD/WELDON TRANNIES

It would be difficult to read A. B. 'Banjo' Paterson's epic poem 'The Man from Snowy River' without being stirred and inspired by the exploits of those hard-riding horsemen of Australia's high country. But are these free-spirited men who have captured the imagination of generations of Australians merely characters of the past, or do they continue to ride the hillsides today?

At least one family continues the traditions of horsemanship that Paterson so lovingly described in his classic poem. The Pendergasts live in the Snowy Mountains, New South Wales, and when it comes to equalling the daring exploits of the riders of long ago, it would be hard to find a better example. Their ancestors came to the region in 1830, and many Pendergasts have since been born and raised in these highlands. They have never known a life without horses, but sadly, the days of horsemanship are slowly coming to a close. Charlie Byrne, whose mother was a Pendergast, has had to turn to other work to make a living. He is now working on the main roads, but the change saddens him. 'I really miss [the old life], you know. It's turned from horses to machines, and that's not my way of life; but we still have to earn a living.'

They may no longer work with their beloved horses, but Noel Pendergast and his friends and family, still ride with great skill. When a celebration is imminent, that is a family gathering with a picnic race, the Pendergasts go off on a wild horse round-up, riding the hillsides in search of the wild brumbies that roam the area. The riders know their country well, and how to find the horses. As Noel says, 'In this country the brumbies eat a lot of the bark off the trees, the box bark, and if you can find a tree that's been freshly eaten, you know you're getting close. Then you find the tracks, and once you get on to the fresh tracks, you're home and hosed.'

The riders eagerly anticipate these 'celebration days'; it is not often that they have a chance to ride like this. It is a wild dash through beautiful country — through thickly wooded slopes, across open alpine meadows and over icy highland streams. Skilful horsemanship is needed to ride through the densely

Above and opposite. *Men like the Pendergasts keep alive the tradition of 'Banjo' Paterson's poem 'The Man from Snowy River'.*

Overleaf: *Wild brumby horses offer the pursuing horsemen a test of skill and endurance.*
WELDON TRANNIES

The excitement of the race is experienced by both man and horse.
The riding is daring, requiring skilful horsemanship.

packed gum trees, and to catch the wild, unpredictable brumbies. It is dangerous and daring, but all the riders are more than capable.

When the day of the round-up arrives, hooves pound the earth and manes fly as the riders weave in and out of the trees in pursuit of the wild horses. The chase is fast and furious as the Pendergasts test their skill against the pure energy of the brumbies. By the end of the day they will have rounded up a group of wild animals that will pace within the unaccustomed confines of stockyards.

The men will not be able to help but show their elation and pleasure after one of these musters. One old timer, Norman McGussiche, recalls after one ride: 'It's a pity we didn't have the old boys — Jimmy loved it here. Wouldn't 'e be excited over this turnout; in fact it's stirred me up.'

Once the wild horses have been caught, roped and led home, the Pendergasts have a few days in which to break in the brumbies, turning them into mounts for the family reunion race.

When the great day arrives, excitement fills the air as the announcer's voice is heard across the makeshift racetrack, and men and women line their horses up at the starting post. 'Now ladies and gentlemen, we have the main race of the day — The Man from Snowy River brumby race. All the horses taking part in this race have been mustered out of the Snowy Mountains.'

The running of the race is a proud moment for the Pendergast family. They have proved that even if the mountain rider's way of life has disappeared, they still have the skill of their forefathers, those men of Snowy River. Today's Snowy Mountain riders are keeping the legend alive, showing that the horsemen of the past are not just characters in the lines of a poem. Banjo Paterson, the man who began the legend, should have the last word about men like the Pendergasts:

'It was grand to see that mountain horseman ride.'

THE DRIVERS

Helicopter pilots with hard hats and stereo music headphones are far from the image most people have of Aussie stockmen, who traditionally are tanned and wiry young riders with battered Akubras jammed on their heads, wheeling their horses around fallen logs in the northern cattle country. But a new breed of stockmen has arrived. Called the 'Drivers', these spaceage musterers have helicopters instead of steeds. They rise and fall and spin around the vast cattle properties, flying where in the past even the best of the riders have been unable to go.

Heli-mustering is mustering with a difference. It is not cheap and it is not easy. The pilots spend up to ten hours in the air rounding up cattle previously lost and left to roam wild in inaccessible country, and clearing paddocks of old scrub bulls that have evaded the horseback stockmen for years. John Weymouth, who runs a mustering company, says that 'Even experienced pilots find that they do not know everything, and some can make very expensive mistakes.'

Tony Ferris found out just how expensive these mistakes can be when his helicopter crashed in the bush. After surveying the wreckage, he realised instinctively that the new stockmen are like their horseback counterparts who must get back on their horses after a bad fall and make sure that they still have their nerve. According to Tony, 'It is a matter of getting back into a helicopter straight away and flying around for a while.'

The drivers will do any job anywhere in the Northern Territory at a moment's notice. All the men have to do, it seems, is know cattle and fly a helicopter. This may sound easy, but as John Weymouth points out. 'Pilots need to be aware of the dangers involved. With their position in relation to objects such as trees constantly changing, concentration and split-second timing are often vital. As well, they need to be in tune with the cattle so that they can anticipate their every move.'

John Weymouth is experienced in giving helicopter pilots the extra training necessary to turn them into airborne stockmen. He subsidises the training of some of his heli-musterers, but most are prepared to pay their own expenses. A year is spent in training for the special

Above. *Helicopters make modern mustering faster and more efficient.*
Overleaf. *To the sound of a chopper's blades, Northern Territory buffalo are driven through the swamps.*
WELDON TRANNIES

WELDON TRANNIES

WELDON TRANNIES

The forlorn looking face of a Territory buffalo.

demands of the job, which often involves some hair-raising risks.

Student stockmen have included people from diverse backgrounds such as a former United States Navy pilot and a twenty-one-year-old horseriding stockman who saw the need to embrace the new technology that is plucking riders from their saddles. Eric Webb, a young stockman, saved $10,000 to train for and become one of the new outback elite.

Although some of the older stockmen are not impressed by the high-flying cowboys, George Dunn, head stockman at the vast Wave Hill cattle station, agrees that they have their place. Without them, the wild bulls would spend longer in the protective hills, thus lowering the breeding standards. Mustered by rotor, the wild bulls can be replaced by stud bulls to maintain beef quality.

Heli-mustering also makes possible the testing of the cattle for tuberculosis. All the cattle, including the wild bulls, need to be tested in order to prevent the disease from spreading.

On the large Victoria River Downs station, a final muster of the elusive bulls before the wet season begins can make or break the new breed of flying stockmen. They stop only to refuel or take a quick lunch. The rest of a long day is spent in the air, confronting wild cattle that have never seen humans, and have eluded capture for up to ten years.

It is important that at a pre-dawn conference the fliers agree on a co-ordinated plan, then keep in constant contact with each other. As they duck, weave, bob and charge, these heli-musterers always have in mind that they must 'tuck in', that is, push the wild cattle into a mob, and keep them there. In over eight hours of hard flying, they hope to round up 1,200 head of cattle, but if only one bull breaks away, the whole herd will follow and the drivers could lose a thousand cattle in the hills for another year.

Heli-mustering is dangerous with the possibility of crashing being ever present. Yet Tony Ferris, who did just that, thinks the agricultural fliers in their fixed-wing planes take greater risks. He believes that the pilots have a better chance of surviving a crash, but admits falling out of the sky is worse than falling off a horse!

The Drivers have become an integral part of the Australian Outback scene. Out in the mustering camps, the billy still boils for the welcome smoko breaks, but the new breed of stockmen is providing some new bushman's yarns. When flyboys doss down with cowboys at the end of the muster, the tales grow taller as the flights of Outback fancy assume new heights.

Heli-mustering can be dangerous, and the pilots' mistakes expensive, as this crashed helicopter indicates.

WELDON TRANNIES

*Once the buffalo have been rounded up into
an enclosure, the helicopter pilot's work is done.*

GUNTHER DEICHMANN/WELDON TRANNIES

Above. *Heli-mustering can be a difficult and
dangerous job, as the helicopter pilots turn and manoeuvre
their machines and fly low to keep the
animals together.*

Left: *Many of the buffalo are
wild and without the use of helicopters may
have evaded capture for as long as ten years.*

MONTE CRISTO

Like many of the townspeople of Junee in southern New South Wales, Reg and Olive Ryan believed their house 'Monte Cristo' was haunted. The name evokes a sense of the supernatural.

The original homestead was extended soon after it was built in 1870s. The resulting grand mansion sits alone on a hill above the town. The Ryans discovered the house in the 1950s — a rundown, vandalised shell with all traces of the delicate cast iron balconies destroyed. There were no doors or windows, and no electricity or water, but the Ryans could see its potential as their future home. Although the previous owners had not seen the house for twenty years, they still imagined it as it was in its heyday. It took the Ryans eight years to convince them to sell it, and at its depreciated value. Finally, they won the ruin for two thousand dollars.

As soon as the Ryans moved in, the haunting began. The whole atmosphere of the house created an uneasy feeling. Situated in an isolated spot out of town, Monte Cristo's soft Victorian charm by day became eerie by night. The moonlight played tricks with the mist and clouds, shadows were cast on the balconies and the stillness of the countryside created a sense of loneliness.

Reg recalls a moment in the early days when 'I was sitting out on the front verandah in broad daylight. There was no cast iron or anything up on the balcony, and with boards missing, I could see up under it. I heard a woman's footsteps ... walking from one room right around the balcony to the other room. But I did not go and have a look because there was no one else at home and I knew there could not be anyone up there.'

Olive Ryan also remembers an odd experience: 'I was sitting in the lounge sewing. I felt somebody put their hand on my shoulder and I looked around but there was no-one there.' She adds: 'When the children were smaller, they used to see faces at the window.'

Reg and Olive worked on Monte Cristo, restoring it to the point where the beautiful mansion has won tourism awards. They open their doors once a year for a great ball that brings people from as far away as Sydney and Melbourne. Old coaches clatter up the gravel drive and disgorge guests dressed in period finery. The guests

Monte Cristo, the beautiful old haunted house near Junee, New South Wales, is the home of Reg and Olive Ryan. Their love for this mansion has survived many disturbing supernatural experiences.

Once a year, Monte Cristo hosts a glittering ball when guests dress in period costumes to match the mansion's grandeur.

definitely a lot of violence in here. There was a girl here who was murdered. She could not have been much more than sixteen, and the body was dragged out there.' He gestured toward the balcony.

According to Liz James, there was the spirit of a bitter, angry old woman who does not like her home being a museum. Suddenly Liz prowled and paused, wrestling with some unseen problem. She was hustled from the darkened room to the shadowy balcony where she collapsed (Van explained that the spirit had entered Liz.) Moments later, she shouted 'I have you now! I have beaten you completely. You will not get away with this. It is no good crying . . .' Then she lapsed into unconsciousness. 'What happened?' asked Liz when she came to. 'It was the old lady,' said Van. 'The old lady was here with us.'

The theatrical behaviour of the mediums was no more strange than the weird experiences the Ryans had already experienced. But Reg and Olive Ryan still live in Monte Cristo, running a successful antique business and welcoming tourists. They challenge the past, yet, says Reg, 'We still have the odd brush with the supernatural.'

Perhaps if you are passing through Junee, Monte Cristo is worth a visit.

dance in a kaleidoscope of colour till well past the witching hour. As the guests travel down the hill again all that can be heard are the sounds of coach wheels gradually diminishing in the distance.

Reg and Olive relate stories of Monte Cristo's darker past. According to Reg, 'There was a mentally retarded lad chained up here for something like thirty or forty years. When his mother died, the tradesmen found him. They found the mother who had been dead a couple of days — the boy was still chained up.' Olive once found a mutilated cat in the kitchen, but 'there was no way anything could have got in.'

The townspeople of Junee had often talked of suicide and murder at Monte Cristo so Reg and Olive decided to test the apparent haunting of their home. They called in Liz James and Van Blore, two mediums, to conduct an exorcism, along with photographer John Murray.

'Please,' cajoled Van Blore as he catfooted around an upstairs room at Monte Cristo, 'things are alright. We are not harming anybody. We want to help. We want to do the right thing.' Around the antique bed, the heavy drapery hung unruffled. Van confided that 'There is

Monte Cristo's elegantly restored Victorian dining room.

MYSTERY OF ZANONI

TERRY DREW

Above. *Underneath the bow of the* Zanoni.

Opposite. *The rudder* (top right) *is still upright, intact and fixed to the stern post.*

Since Australia was first discovered by Europe's intrepid mariners in the 1600s, its treacherous coastal waters have been claiming ships and lives in great numbers. It was, however, a comparatively recent disaster that became one of the nation's greatest mysteries.

In 1867, in Gulf St Vincent, South Australia, a three-masted barque met its fate when a fierce storm suddenly tore apart a clear blue midday sky. In only eight minutes, the barque sank. One moment the crew were trying to obey orders to take in the topsail, and the next moment the ship was on its beam end. Amazingly, every member of the crew survived.

Only the cook and cabin boy were in the galley at the time of the storm. The boy hauled the cook out of the sinking vessel and they clung to an upturned longboat. It took two hours to right the longboat, but only eight minutes to lose their 343-tonne ship.

Zanoni, laden with wheat, had gone. Every member of the crew knew exactly where the ship had gone down as the details were clearly documented, but despite a three-week search by other ships not a trace of *Zanoni* was found. Everybody knew that on its short voyage down the gulf from Port Adelaide *Zanoni* had disappeared near the Long Spit Light, which marked a treacherous sandbar, but no one could find it. A reward was offered, but there were no takers.

It was the beginning of a mystery that ended more than one hundred years later with another freak of nature. Fish provided the vital clue.

The successful searchers, Ian O'Donnell, a computer programmer and underwater explorer, and John McGovern, a former abalone diver and now a prominent Gulf businessman, were simply the latest in a succession of hopeful mystery solvers. They had been

BILL GEOFFREY

Ian O'Donnell and John McGovern spent twelve determined years searching South Australia's Gulf St Vincent
for the wreck of the Zanoni. *Eventually, with the aid of a $2000 reward,*
they solved the mystery and located what became known as South Australia's best preserved wreck.
Their best clue was the presence of large numbers of fish, normally found only around a reef,
and not in this area. With the help of local ex-fisherman, Rex Tyrell, they found the false reef—the Zanoni.

obsessed by *Zanoni* for twelve years, and had studied every available piece of information. For them, there had always been something special about the lost ship, which was the only composite ship wrecked off the South Australian coast. Ian and John had studied details of the ship's design, examined reports of its sinking, and were as aware as everyone else of the exact location. But *Zanoni* was not to be found.

After twelve fruitless years, they were rereading the archives and following the all-too-familiar words, when a tiny piece of information suddenly came into focus. It was a brief mention of the Long Spit Light. The light had been moved three nautical miles since the sinking! It was their best clue yet, but still it was not enough. They needed more leads.

Another lead, even though small, came as a result of John hearing talk of a secret fishing ground known only to four or five fishermen who reckoned they caught

more and bigger snapper there than anywhere else in the gulf. But would these fishermen give details? Not a chance. Fishermen treasure their favourite spots.

John decided to bait his own hook, so to speak. He started by offering a reward of five hundred dollars for information about the fishing ground, but there were no bites. Confident of his angling ability, he advertised several times, the lure finally reaching two thousand dollars. This proved to be irresistible for an old fisherman by the name of Rex Tyrell, who found his memory jogged by John's dangling bait. He remembered a spot he had last fished with great success twelve years ago. By rights there should have been a reef to explain the bountiful harvest but none was charted.

Rex contacted John and Ian, and they quickly arranged to take him out into the gulf waters that had concealed *Zanoni* for so long. At eighty-two, Rex found that his memory had clouded after twelve years, and

MARC FALLANDER

BILL GEOFFREY

TERRY DREW

*After more than 100 years of lying at the bottom of the ocean, the Zanoni and her fittings
and equipment were in remarkably good condition. Numerous diving forays have recovered many items from the fated ship,
such as these plates (left), some historical pieces (top right) and a piece of nautical equipment (above right).
Sadly, sufficient funds are still not available to raise the entire wreck and restore it for public exhibition.*

several promising locations were marked without success. After four hours, and with light fading, it seemed they had undertaken yet another fruitless search — a hunt for a little iron needle in a large haystack.

Before they dejectedly returned to land, the searchers were willing to give Rex one last try. Rex was feeling stirrings of familiarity — the memories of an old fisherman's best catch. The water was nine fathoms deep and only ten minutes of usable daylight remained, apart from the fact that this was the home of the great white shark. They anchored, and John McGovern and another friend dived into the water while Ian took compass bearings.

The pair were underwater only for a short while. When they surfaced, John's cry told the story: 'You bloody beauty! That's it! That's it!' They were laughing and cheering and shouting 'We've done it! It's the whole ship. It's unbelievable! We've hit the jackpot!'

It was indeed a jackpot, later to be described as the best-preserved wreck ever to be found in South Australian waters. Under normal circumstances, waterlogged wheat would have expanded to three times its volume, and *Zanoni* should have been blown apart by her cargo. As it was, only the midship section had collapsed, probably due to the swelling of the wheat. Many of her fittings, equipment and crew's possessions were intact and have now been recovered. Unfortunately, there has not been enough money to bring *Zanoni* to the surface for exhibition.

There have been diving vandals too, although cruising sharks have kept many away. The sharks have been attracted by the influx of fishing boats coming for the bounty of fat snapper, the tell-tale snapper that finally provided nature's clue to a century-old mystery that began with an eight-minute reign of stormy terror.

EIGHTEEN FOOTERS

ACTION GRAPHICS

Sydney Harbour is universally regarded as a unique and beautiful body of water. Captain Cook, on his voyage of discovery in 1770, sailed right past it, not realising that there was such a large body of water beyond the deceptively narrow headlands of the harbour. Eighteen years later, however, a desperate Captain Arthur Phillip edged HMS *Sirius* through the Heads to discover the vast sheltered waterway and a likely location for a British penal settlement.

Despite the huge open waterway scalloped around the edges by numerous palm-fringed bays, recreation was the last consideration for the tough sailors and soldiers, and the convicts brought by Captain Phillip from a harsh penal system half a world away. If only they could have imagined that seventy-seven years later another Englishman would arrive on these sunny shores and provide the basis for a sport that would not only be uniquely Australian, but would also belong to Sydney Harbour itself.

Eighteen-footer yacht racing was introduced to Sydney Harbour in 1865 by Mark Foy, who was also to found one of the nation's greatest retail chains. He came to Australia as a free man, with a passion for sailing. He brought to Sydney the first eighteen-footer yacht, a sleek and swift little vessel that shocked the more conservative colonists.

In the 1890s, Mark Foy was not popular among his colleagues at the Sydney Flying Yacht Squadron, who would not let him bring in a narrower beam required for eighteen-footers. So, in order to break free of oversalted traditions, in 1935 Mark Foy formed the New South Wales Eighteen-Foot Sailing Club.

Above and opposite. *Eighteen footers have graced Sydney Harbour since the 1890s and have evolved from the early ten-man crewed yachts to the fast, streamlined models of today.*

ACTION GRAPHICS

In their quest for speed, eighteen-footer crews spend more time out of the boat than in it.
The Hooker's crew perform some precarious acrobatics to fight off the opposition.

Eighteen footers are the fastest open-boat racers on the water, reaching up to thirty knots under full sail. They have a light hull, thirty inches (76 centimetres) wide with an eight foot (2.5 metre) beam on an open centreboard. Initially, ten crew were needed to sail an eighteen-footer yacht, the number dropped to eight, then to six, and finally to the three of today.

When Sydneysiders chance upon the harbour on a Sunday, they cannot help being captivated by the sight of these seemingly flimsy vessels tearing across the water. As one club official boasts: 'They are so spectacular, so fast!'

Eighteen footers are very expensive, at around $100,000, and sponsorship from major companies is difficult to attract for this type of boat. As for the yachts, their butterfly lightness and flutter of speed are truly indicative of their brief but colourful existence. An eighteen-footer lasts only a year. The stress of speed on the light wings and mast is a guarantee of impermanence.

Opposite. Sydney's eighteen footers are fast, exciting *and expensive. Around $100,000 will cover the cost of building the yacht and keeping it in the water for one year of first class racing.*

The prohibitive costs of the boats and the unwillingness of the major sponsors to send their advertising dollar to the smaller centres, has made eighteen-foot yacht racing predominantly a Sydney Harbour sport. Any interstate competition usually involves the used boats from Sydney — the darting champions of Sydney that have had their year of glory, and are sold to keen racers in Brisbane or Victoria.

Competitive series have also been held in France and San Francisco, the latter arising from a citizen of the Bay City seeing a race and, in the words of a Sydney club official, 'being besotted'. The only real competition, however, comes from Australia's nearest neighbours, the New Zealanders. In Auckland, the Kiwis have taken the World Championship from the Aussies seven times. Sydney sailors suggest, with just a touch of acrimony, that it is because the Kiwis know their own waters better. In truth, there is no denying the sheer Australianness of eighteen-footer racing — and that its true centre is Sydney Harbour.

Costs and continuing changes to the little fliers have been a threat to this class of yacht racing, but tougher rules are at work to ensure the survival of a spectacle which would have been unimaginable to those aboard HMS *Sirius* two hundred years ago.

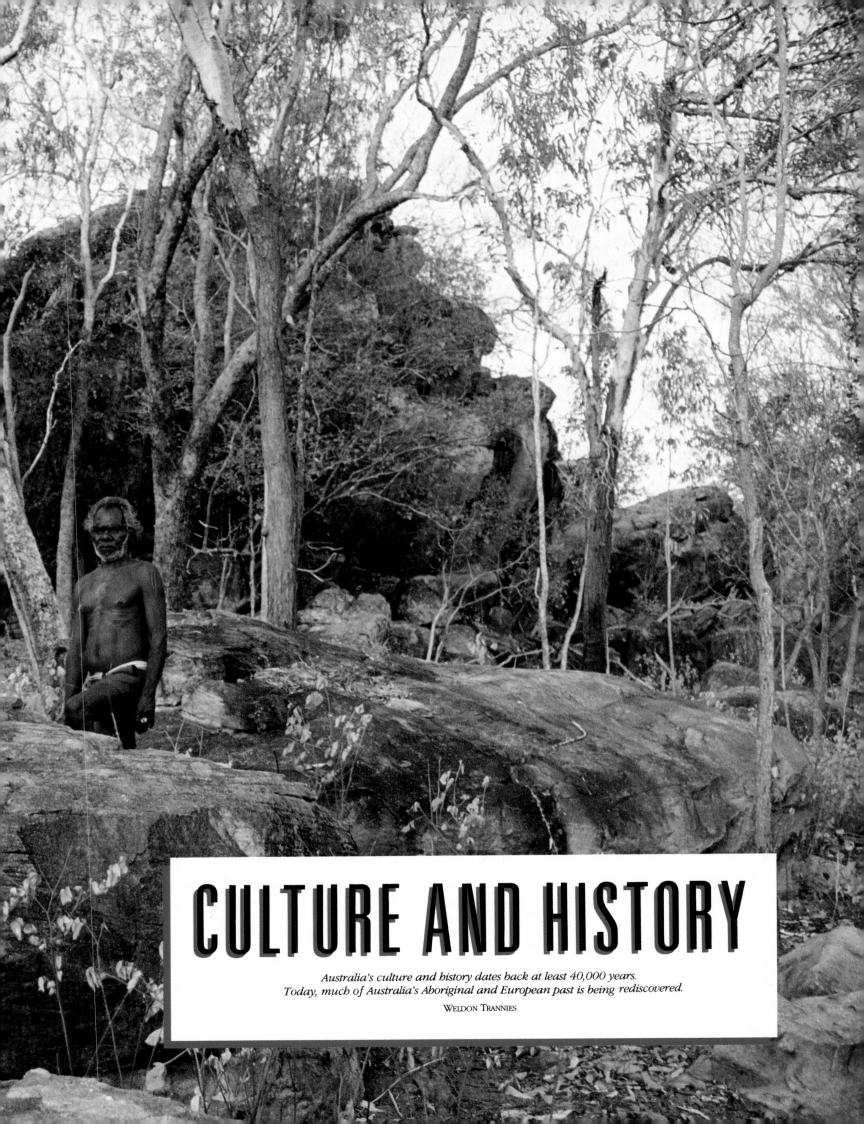

CULTURE AND HISTORY

Australia's culture and history dates back at least 40,000 years.
Today, much of Australia's Aboriginal and European past is being rediscovered.

WELDON TRANNIES

CLAUDE COIRAULT

apparently barren land well and are able to find sixty edible vegetable plants and thirty varieties of fruits and seeds. Yet, as spokesman Harry Wilson says, 'We need tea and sugar and flour. We've been taught by Europeans to have these things. We can't get out of it now but we still want to do our own thing.'

At Peppimenarti, the Aborigines have amalgamated the ancient and the modern. Stockmen round up the cattle in four-wheel-drive vehicles and teachers teach young Aborigines European action songs, such as 'Simple Simon says—clap your hands'. But later, in the dusty shade of trees not far from that classroom, the old and honoured storyteller Mirramook gives the same children her treasury of tales and traditions from the Dreamtime.

This is all part of a most unusual pioneering venture. Now Aborigines are able to take control of their future, no longer bound to the mission stations or virtual prisoners of their own land held by Europeans, nor, at worst, condemned to a life in the seedier streets of towns and cities.

At Peppimenarti, especially, they have made the most of opportunity. For a while, they even banned welfare payments to themselves. 'No work, no money' was the policy. The fluctuating national economy, however, brought the need for compromise but it was no compromise in pride. As Harry Wilson pointed out, the Europeans were no longer 'boss'. Power now lay with the elders, as in traditional Aboriginal society.

During the Aboriginal ritual of male circumcision, the young initiate cries out in pain—cries covered each time by a cacophony of shouts by a shielding circle of men. The ceremonial cut, however, is not as deep as the love that follows—all the men being eager to take the new young man to their hearts by clasping and embracing him. This reaching out is the most touching moment of several days of celebration. This is a ceremony regaining its rightful place in an ancient culture.

At Peppimenarti, in the northwest of the Northern Territory, ceremonial life and tradition go hand in hand with modern European culture. The area was reclaimed by Aborigines under a new law in 1976 enabling them to return legally to traditional lands. It is a cattle station with an office, computers and other modern coveniences. The Aborigines who came to the area from the towns, the missions and the stock camps were determined to make the most of the European world but still maintain and strengthen their ancient culture.

Australian Aborigines have the oldest continuous culture in the world. At Peppimenarti, the homes have electricity and modern conveniences, but the women still choose to stick-scrape the earth for food roots and catch turtles for a healthy diet. They know this

Above. *Witchetty grubs are found in the roots of* Acacia kempeana *bushes in central Australia and are a valuable staple in the Aboriginal diet.*
Above left and opposite. *Aborigines from Peppimenarti station maintain their Aboriginal traditions and customs, often attending initiation ceremonies and important meetings of clans and groups great distances away.*

Claude Coirault

CLAUDE COIRAULT

Above and opposite. *The rich colours and intricate patterns of traditional styles are the inspiration for much of today's painting at Peppimenarti, and the children grow up with a keen respect for their ancient culture.*

Claire Leimbach

Claude Coirault

Top. *Aboriginal women have their own special ceremonies.*
Above. *Sturt's desert pea provides a splash of red in the brown desert.*

CLAUDE COIRAULT

Peppimenarti women pass on tribal knowledge to their children.

CARMEN KY

At Peppimenarti, Aborigines can return to their traditional lifestyle, while still enjoying the conveniences of the 1980s. Cooking turtle in a campfire contrasts with trucks, deep freezers and the use of computers at the station's office.

The people of Peppimenarti must participate in ceremonies. Some of them live 1,100 kilometres away in the desert. The Europeans used to call it 'going walkabout', and labelled Aboriginal workers as irresponsible when they suddenly walked off the job into the distant haze. In fact, those 'irresponsible' disappearances were made by tribal members who were determined, despite early European restrictions, to maintain their complex culture. Now, Aborigines find it easier to travel by truck—their own truck from their own cattle station—to the often distant secret and important ceremonies.

Peppimenarti itself has become a centre for ceremonial life, especially for the ritual of circumcision, the entry of boys into manhood. Every two years,

hundreds of people travel to the station. There is feasting, the renewing of friendships and dancing. For women, there are also special ceremonies. Girls who may spend their day at a computer in the station office can be seen in special dress being guided by older women around the seated men. The girls become guardians of secrets regarding behaviour and tribal law.

The gathering culminates with the male ceremony. As boys are 'seized' and forced away from their mothers, there is an element of sheer symbolism. While the boys are kept secluded, the dancing continues, but on the following days, the boys are brought back to watch. The next morning, the boys return to the site of the final ceremony, and, riding astride their elders piggyback style, they make stately progress to within fifty paces of

CLAIRE LEIMBACH

Aboriginal children at Peppimenarti can learn about and understand the importance of Aboriginal traditions and customs while at the same time benefiting from a European style education.

the waiting relatives. The young initiates are encircled by a tight group of men to shield them from the eyes of the women and children. The cutting implement drops towards the boys and with each cut, a loud cry goes up from the circle to drown any sound. The boy emerges as a man, holder of the secrets of Aboriginal society. It is a proud, if briefly painful, moment for a young man, now seen with new eyes by his mother who loosened her hold only days ago. It has been this way for thousands of years, interrupted only by missionaries and government authorities whose bans almost caused the loss of this ancient knowledge that is now fully revived.

The Aborigines of Peppimenarti have chosen to live with the best of both worlds. In 1976 Peppimenarti was isolated and empty, except for the stray cattle in the bush. Backed by the rich texture of an almost forgotten culture, the people of Peppimenarti began building their community. The road was not sealed, but the huge cattle transports coming and going in clouds of red dust gave them a start. Then came an airstrip, school, clinic, houses and a store, together with work and pride.

Peppimenarti is a kind of mental condominium— where the idea of electronic computation of sales figures lives comfortably side by side with the ubiquitous anthill, believed, from the Dreamtime, to be the captured forms of the innocent children of adulterous women. Aboriginal tribal law embodies strict codes of behaviour that enable the people to join together with a common purpose—to make a success of their lives on their own land.

EVERY DOT GENTLY AND CAREFULLY

CARMEN KY

The Papunya settlement lies west of Alice Springs, in the beautiful MacDonnell Ranges.

It is a long and an unusual journey from a small Aboriginal settlement north of the ancient weathered rocks of Central Australia's MacDonnell Ranges to the fashionable art galleries of London, Paris and New York. But it is a journey that has been made by the acclaimed dot paintings of the Papunya Tula artists, whose art has intrigued and excited the international art world.

Papunya, 258 kilometres west of Alice Springs, was established in 1960 in an attempt to assimilate the Aborigines of the Western Desert into the European way of life. The settlement brought people out of their traditional desert homelands of sandhills and spinifex into an environment of concrete and corrugated iron—what one of the Papunya artists calls 'chicken houses'. For the Aborigines, the transition was a break from the close affinity with their land, which was the source of their artistic, cultural and spiritual inspiration, and a decline in the traditional expression of their legends.

All that changed in 1971, when Sydneysider Geoff Bardon, an art and craft teacher at Papunya settlement's school, suggested that his pupils liven up the bare school walls with a mural. He did not realise that his suggestion was unleashing a torrent of artistic talent. The mural project sparked off unprecedented enthusiasm among adults as well as children and, before long, the elders were enthusiastically creating their own mural. Geoff had rekindled a suppressed interest in the traditional art and heritage of the Papunya people, and the men soon began to paint individually on anything that they could obtain—on canvas and on box sides. This was the beginning of the successful Papunya co-operative.

To Aborigines, painting is just one link in a complex chain of storytelling, songs, corroborees, legends and the passing on of information to the next generation. These are all manifestations of the

CLAUDE COIRAULT

Lucy Naparulla of Mt Allen completing a painting in the Papunya art style.

Dreamtime, the Aboriginal understanding of the world. The Papunya artists are inspired by the land from which they have sprung; a land crisscrossed with dreaming trails that is therefore sacred. Their art tells a story of men on journeys, water sources, game, ancestral figures and land features. It tells of the land's history and geography, in two-dimensional abstract designs that show little concern for the visual reality that the European eye demands. Papunya artists paint stylised designs that represent men sitting around a fire, eating bush tucker, or the tracks of a wallaby as it crosses sandhills or passes a waterhole. To the unaccustomed eye, the paintings are merely attractive patterns, but the initiated read the canvas like a map—a two-dimensional landscape, painted from a bird's eye point of view.

Right. *Dot paintings cover the walls of the Araluen Arts Centre in Alice Springs.*

CARMEN KY

REG MORRISON/WELDON TRANNIES

It is a painstaking technique that requires concentration and a steady hand. 'It is a very slow job,' artist Michael Nelson Juddamurra explains. 'If you are a good artist, well you have to make sure that you place every dot gently and very carefully.' And this is exactly what Nelson and his fellow Papunya artists do. Using acrylic paints, they slowly and methodically dab a stick into paint, and take it from paint to canvas. In a striking blend of earth colours, black, white, red and ochre, their paintings take shape, and tell ancient stories of the Dreamtime; the dreaming of the honey ant, the possum, the old man and the child.

The tales may be old but the dot technique and the materials are still developing and changing. No longer reliant only on the bare ground, the growing band of artists demand stretched canvas and paints brought to Papunya by willing helpers.

Top. *Placing every dot 'gently and carefully'.*

Right. *Maxie Tjampitjinpa, one of the second generation of Papunya Tula artists.*

Opposite. *An artist uses a stone to mix paint.*

CLAUDE COIRAULT

168

CLAUDE COIRAULT

Encouraged by teacher Geoff Bardon, the Papunya Tula art movement began in the early 1970s and has progressed to high standards. To the uninitiated, the flat, two-dimensional designs are little more than patterns, but to the Aboriginal artists, the painting is an interpretation of their surroundings, culture and legends.
Opposite. *Eunice Napangardi,* Uparli Dreaming. *Papunya dot paintings such as these hang in galleries around the world and fetch high prices from eager buyers. The money received by the artist often finds its way back to the community and is used to encourage other artists to develop this art form.*

Men such as Nelson and Maxie Tjampitjinpa are the second wave of the Papunya Tula artists' movement. The elders—grandfathers, fathers and uncles—have passed on their knowledge to the younger men. Nelson Tjampitjinpa is continuing his family tradition. 'When I paint,' he says, 'I think very hard about what they have taught me and shown me on the ground . . . I do the same, just as they taught me.' Hopefully, this creative compulsion will continue to be handed down to future generations and, inspired by traditional songs, dances and storytelling, the art of the Western Desert will endure.

As sophisticated art lovers view these vibrant earthy canvases, both small and large, simple and epic, they have little idea of the motivation and inspiration of the people who paint them. It is to be hoped that the worldwide interest that the Papunya artists have aroused is the beginning of a true understanding and appreciation of Aboriginal art.

Meanwhile, back in Papunya, as the acclaim and prizes roll in, there also comes a more tangible and vital reward. The money received for the art of men such as Nelson is essential to keep their art alive and to ensure that younger men are instructed in interpreting the subtle relationship between the land and the people that live on it. The money also brings hope, as Nelson says, for improvement of the lot of his people, bringing them the rewards they richly deserve.

THE CONTRACT

Percy Trezise met Dick Goodala Thaldin at the site of an empty swimming pool at Karumba in the eastern corner of the Gulf of Carpentaria. Percy was busy painting a mermaid on the pool floor when Dick accosted him with that familiar greeting—'G'day Mate!' Beneath Dick's laconic smile lay a well-thought out plan to work with Percy whose paintings of the Australian bush evoke an immediate sense of recognition. The plan was destined to come to fruition.

Dick Goodala Thaldin, the Lardil clansman from Mornington Island off the far north coast of Australia, was later to become known as Dick Roughsey. His work would hang in homes and galleries throughout Australia and overseas.

Dick told Percy that he wanted to paint—to be a better painter than Albert Namatjira. Namatjira, whose Arrernte watercolours of central Australia have always been highly-prized, was Dick's hero. When Dick learned that Percy was an artist, he was determined to meet him as a step towards realising his dream of becoming a painter himself.

When Trezise and Roughsey met, Dick was already married, living with his wife and six children on Mornington Island. There, he was known as The Big Man of Two Worlds, the Aboriginal and the European. In his 'first world' he suffered, as many Aborigines did, from trachoma. This disease of the eye made him painfully sensitive to bright light.

Percy Trezise and Dick Roughsey discovered together far north Queensland's magnificent Quinkan rock art galleries, a veritable treasurehouse of Aboriginal art. Albert Namatjira was Dick Roughsey's hero, but Dick was also a talented artist who developed his own style of painting.

Percy Trezise

Dick Roughsey with a bark painting. Dick was originally from Mornington Island but settled in north Queensland, and became not only a well-known painter, but also the Chairman of the Aboriginal Arts Board. Dick was unusual in that he lived in two worlds, remaining close to his tribal ties, but also fitting into the white man's world.

Again, like so many Aboriginal children, Dick was taken from his parents when he was eight to be given a 'better life' by missionaries. His schoolwork was so good that other children copied from him. His teachers did not want him to leave, but at the age of twelve, he returned to his parents and the bush. He became a man of two worlds, handling both cultures with ease. From behind the protective tint of sunglasses, Dick immersed himself in the colours and shapes of his country.

From their first meeting, an extraordinary 'contract' was to evolve between Percy Trezise and Dick Roughsey. Percy was impressed by the sheer enthusiasm of Dick who said he later laughed at those early 'attempts', which reflected the heritage of thousands of years of traditional Aboriginal painting. They sold well, but Dick wanted to emulate his hero, the great Namatjira, and eventually to go beyond watercolours with oils and

acrylics. He began creating his own vision of the landscape, often including impressionistic but vivid figures of his own people. Dick visited Percy's home in Cairns, benefiting from his new friend and benefactor's advice, which helped him to refine his work. Later Dick became chairman of the Aboriginal Arts Board, and his relationship with Percy entered a new and vital phase.

Percy had been a commercial pilot with an Australian domestic airline. His flying skills were called into play when he decided he wanted to locate ancient Aboriginal art. With Dick aboard, he flew long and low over 10,000 square kilometres of the sandstone cliffs and spectacular gorges of the Quinkan area in southeast Cape York Peninsula, seeking likely 'gallery' sites. Together, they found hundreds of galleries, some more than 30 metres long. The history of the Aborigines could be seen in the sequential styles covering thousands of years. Many galleries had never been rediscovered by Aborigines who were afraid of spirits, or by white men riding who had never bothered to dismount to uncover these treasures. With the best of intentions, Percy set out to achieve two aims: to ensure protection of the galleries and to open their historical beauty to all Australians.

A battle ensued with politicians and public servants telling Trezise to 'stop interfering in Aboriginal affairs'. Dick rallied to help his friend and mentor, throwing the support of the Arts Board behind Percy's fight.

Dick also pressured his own people, saying he wanted to give them back part of what they had lost— their deep cultural heritage. He started teaching them to make cultural artefacts, walking the dry, humming bush with them to choose just the right tree for didjeridus, boomerangs and other items.

While Percy fought for official protection of the land, Dick prepared his people so that they would be able to cope with the expected tourism in a positive way. As Percy pointed out, 'People are entitled to see some of the sites, especially the children, who could be guided by Aborigines to see the vast value of wilderness and art by people of the past and the present.'

Together, Percy Trezise and Dick Roughsey triumphed. In 1976 the land became the Quinkan Reserve, an area of 600 square kilometres where Aboriginal relics are protected. It is a national park that stands as a memorial to thousands of years of Australian culture, and to the black artist and his white colleague who fought for it.

Dick Roughsey was always willing to go anywhere and do anything for his people. He had always wanted to be a figurehead, inspiring people with his own dream, his own achievement. Before he died, he enjoyed simply sitting under a huge mango tree in the dust outside the Quinkan pub, with Percy a few metres away on the verandah, each putting his own vision of the land onto canvas. Eventually, he passed from both worlds he had mastered, to become part of a history for all Australians.

WOMEN OF UTOPIA

HEYTESBURY HOLDINGS LTD

Aboriginal art is the latest sensation in the art world. Paintings, carvings, pottery and screenprints are sold in shops and galleries all over the world, where customers and gallery visitors are fascinated by the unusual and intricate designs. Now another medium is bringing Aboriginal designs into the limelight: fabrics. Aboriginal women from the small settlement of Utopia in the Northern Territory are using fabrics to introduce their timeless art to batik, a craft that is not their own. The craft of batik, imported from Indonesia, has made an unlikely liaison with the traditional art of outback Australia.

Utopia is a small Aboriginal settlement 200 kilometres northeast of Alice Springs. Despite the name's derivation from the sixteenth-century novel by Sir Thomas More, describing a perfect imaginary island, Utopia is no paradise; it is a simple Aboriginal enclave in the inhospitable central desert.

One of Utopia's residents is Rosalie Kunoth-Monks, who became famous for her starring role in the 1950s film *Jedda*. She is now a senior projects officer with the National Aboriginal Development Commission, acting in a supportive role to the women of Utopia who are involved in the art of batik. Through batik she is encouraging the women to develop a new sense of pride as well as financial independence.

Batik's essential materials are white cloth (often silk), wax and dyes. The women are taught to 'draw' on the cloth with melted wax, to create the designs that they know best. Drawing their inspiration from the rugged land, they trace the wax pipe over the cloth, forming patterns that include bush food and flowers, lizards, snakes and other wild animals—designs that are typical of the delicacy and intricacy of any form of Aboriginal art, and qualities that are well suited to the technique of batik.

Above. *The women of Utopia draw their inspiration from the environment to create designs such as this* Emu Hunt and Wild Tomato Awelye *by Anna Petyarre.*

Opposite: *The introduction of the craft of batik has created industry and brought greater independence to the women of Utopia. Their designs are delicate but striking and sell in fashion shops around the world.*

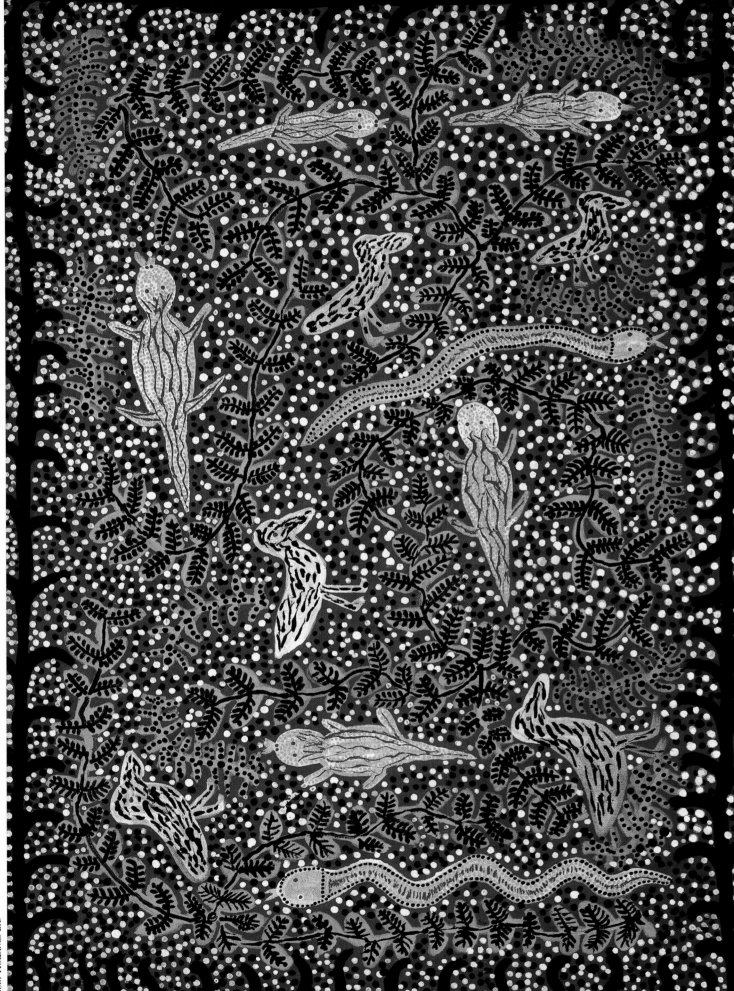

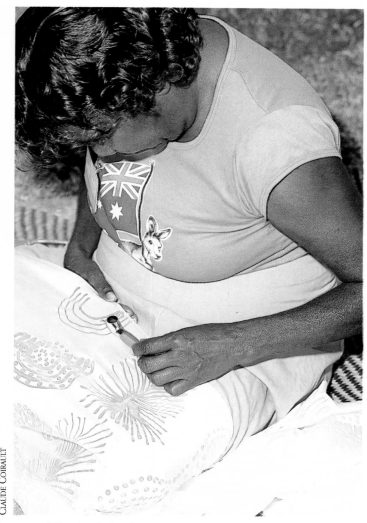

HEYTESBURY HOLDINGS LTD

CLAUDE COIRAULT

Above left. *Eileen Bird's* Wild Orange and Centipede Awelye.
Above right. *Applying the melted wax to the cloth is a delicate operation. The women make colourful designs, based on the food, flowers and animals found in their environment.*
Opposite. *Ruby Kngwarreye's* Blue Tongue Lizard Awelye.

Once the design is created, the cloth is then dyed. Using the most basic utensils—plastic buckets and bowls—the women immerse the fabrics in dyes of many hues: pink, lilac, blue and yellow. The secret of the batik process is that the cloth under the wax remains white. After the first drying, a second or third wax application can be made and the dyeing process is repeated. In this way it is possible to build up a delicate design using two or three overlapping colours and shapes to achieve the final result.

The women enjoy their new occupation, which still enables them to continue their normal daily tasks. They work in their own time, their children playing nearby, and still carry out their tribal duties, such as food gathering. Traditionally, while the men hunt big game, Aboriginal women gather wild fruit and search for delicacies such as lizards and the fat white witchetty grubs that live in acacia wood. They look for many sources of bush food—wild coconuts or the bottlebrush flower, and goannas, which they catch by hand and stun by biting the creature on the back of the head. The women's role is also to teach children where to find food, and most importantly, what is safe to eat. By the age of ten, these children are able to survive if lost in this unforgiving country that has claimed the lives of many bush-ignorant Europeans. Rosalie Kunoth-Monks explains that 'It is a very important task that the women have for the continuation of the law—the law really holds us together and even includes the knowledge of how to cut meat, how to cook it—that is a ritual which must be learned.'

While the cloth is undergoing the drying processes, the women gather their food and the children collect firewood for lunch. It is an informal affair as lizards are roasted and the group sits under the shade of a welcoming tree. With lunch over, it is time to return to the art of batik. Now the fabric is ready for the final stage—boiling the wax out of the cloth. By now, the plain white fabric has been transformed into beautiful patterns of soft colours that will in turn be made up into attractive garments to sell in the fashion shops of Europe, America and Australia. A new and distinctly Australian Aboriginal product has been created by the women of Utopia.

THE WHITE ROSE ORCHESTRA

KANGAROO PRESS

Until recently the White Rose Orchestra was performing four or five nights a week. In earlier days, when Frank was based on his father's farm at rural Binnaway, New South Wales, he took people through waltzes and quicksteps every night, and then got up early to join the family sheep-shearing.

Frank settled at Binnaway, setting up his own recording studio on his farm in the 1970s. The first five long-play recordings were best sellers.

Frank wrote much of the music himself, often from inspirations at most unlikely times, such as when driving his car. A tune would come into his head and when he got home he would play it on the piano and compose a new song. He taped the songs for 'the boys' who would rehearse them for a

FRANK BOURKE RECORDINGS

Frank Bourke, the man who formed the White Rose Orchestra and became the king of the dance hall.

Frank Bourke was only thirteen years old when he first gave the people of rural New South Wales something to dance to back in 1936. He would escape as often as possible from the shearing shed to pound away on the family's upright piano, playing the sort of music people loved to dance to; the one-two-three of 'After the Ball' and the one-two-one-two of 'The Pride of Erin'.

For his first paid performance, he travelled 70 kilometres by horse and sulky and earned three pounds. Only a year later, he composed his first dance-song. 'Everybody learned how to dance in those days,' Frank said, and he was just the boy to provide the music.

He formed a group called the White Rose Orchestra, which hit the road and did not stop travelling and recording until the 1980s. By this time Frank was in his mid-sixties and the oldest group member was in his mid-eighties. 'I'm the man with the old-fashioned dance stand,' goes Frank's theme song, 'It's the band that has travelled the land'—16,000 kilometres a year, in fact.

For a long time Frank kept to his home state of New South Wales, but as his popularity spread and as the other old-time dance bands faded away, the other eastern states called on the White Rose to bring a fragrant air of more elegant times to their country halls. Keen dancers often followed the band, such as the couple who drove from Newcastle to Gundagai, in step with Frank's engagements along the way.

Frank Bourke Recordings

The White Rose Orchestra 'has travelled the land', bringing music throughout the countryside. Playing an assortment of musical instruments, the group continued to entertain and record into the 1980s, when the oldest member of the group was in his mid-eighties. The enthusiasm for dance-hall music has never waned.

couple of months and then record. The songs such as 'Katie is me matey . . .' are not chart busters but their insistent beat has the magical power to raise people from their seats and set them on circular paths around the dance floor. 'It is a gift,' Frank said modestly. 'I love the music and I love that particular type of dance where they can sway and do not have to hurry too much. It is a kind of ballet dance in the way that they enjoy every movement they make.'

Frank never took to rock music. He did not have to, as older people stayed with him, and younger generations took to the siren-songs of the past with equal enjoyment. As a typical old-time dance fan pointed

out, 'He has brought a lot of joy to thousands of people.'

More than fifty years ago, thirteen-year-old Frank Bourke, with the music running through his head, bumped his way across the countryside for his first performance. Now the White Rose Orchestra's records are promoted on television, which was once Frank's dream of the future.

Music styles have changed throughout the years but the music of 'the man with the old-fashioned dance band' has stood the passage of time. Frank Bourke and his White Rose Orchestra continue to entertain both young and old.

EDUCATIONAL EXPERIMENT

Children in Victoria are being offered a unique history lesson that takes them back to the gold rush days of the 1850s. Ballarat's Sovereign Hill project is a faithful reproduction of a prosperous mining town, which brings to life the last century. A private scheme has been initiated by the Ballarat Historical Park Association, which runs Sovereign Hill and, with the support of the Victorian Education Department, brings in groups of schoolchildren to experience, during a two-day program, school in the 1850s style. Two schools are now operating at Sovereign Hill: the Red Hill National School and St Peter's Denominational School. Both use the National System curriculum, as did their original counterparts in the 1850s.

On arrival at Sovereign Hill, the children dress up in clothes of the period, then march into class at the sound of the school bell. For many, the day's history lesson is a surprise. Although most of the children throw themselves into the spirit of the activity, many of them can not quite distinguish between the two worlds and some are not quite certain if it is real or not.

Living out history is not always a pleasant experience. School in the 1850s was dreaded for good reason. Extremely strict discipline, rigorous learning and hard punishment were the order of the day. Teachers were feared, and they, in turn, were terrified of the forbidding and often unjust school inspectors who made surprise visits on behalf of the office of the National System of Education, the forerunner of our state school systems. This was based on the Irish National System. An inspector's displeasure with either school or teacher could result in the withdrawal of the unfortunate teacher's minimal stipend, or at the very least, reduce the teacher to a state of nerves and humiliation.

Above. *Sovereign Hill township, near Ballarat in Victoria, is an authentic recreation of a nineteenth-century mining town, and the location for a new experiment in teaching history to school children. Children are brought to Sovereign Hill to spend two days experiencing life and education 1850s style. Dressed in period costumes, they explore the town and attend lessons in the schoolroom.*

Right. *Little has changed since the 1850s—girls skip while the boys play their own games. Supported by the Victorian Education Department, Sovereign Hill has two schools which offer children the opportunity to experience history.*

Opposite. *This photograph of a country school in the last century is a reminder of the age when children were subjected to very strict discipline and were expected to speak only when spoken to. Attending school in those days was not always a happy experience, but it was a privilege. Many children had little or no education, and only the 'lucky' ones went to school.*

Top. *During their outing to the township, the children explore the town. These boys look longingly through the 1850s bakery window.*
Above. *In the classroom, everything from the ink-stained desks to the map on the wall is authentic.*
Left. *Children play during break outside the Red Hill National School.*

School 1850s style — children sit at long desks and are made to listen intently to the teacher. To ensure that the experience is authentic, they recite arithmetic tables and write on slates.

Opposite. Clarke's grocery store is a treasure trove of utensils, groceries and sweets, and is popular with young visitors at Sovereign Hill.

BALLARAT HISTORICAL PARK ASSOCIATION

A day at Sovereign Hill provides what no books can—a living history lesson.

In the recreated 1850s classroom, today's children learn just how hard school used to be. They sit at long desks, with all age groups crammed into one small, forbidding classroom. The teacher's power is unchallenged and absolute as the children are taken through arithmetic tables, reading lessons and writing practice on wood-framed slates. Punishment and admonishment are dispensed liberally—children are sent to stand in the corner for talking, and others are rapped (lightly) for not sitting up straight. Left-handed children suffer the most. In the days when writing only with the right hand was acceptable, left-handed students suffered the indignity of having the offending hand tied behind their backs. It is little wonder that old school photographs of the era reveal glum and despondent faces. There was little joy in schools run on the stern lines of the Irish National System, where caning was an everyday occurrence.

Life on the mid-nineteenth century goldfields was tough, and even this form of tyrannical education was a privilege. Immigrants who left the poverty of Europe for the rich promises of Australia's goldfields desperately wanted their children to have a better start in the new land and encouraged them to study. This was not easy. Children were dragged from goldfield to goldfield as their parents followed the lure and promise of richer diggings. These children grew up in rough frontier towns all over the continent, surrounded by gambling, swearing, drinking and licentiousness. It was not an environment conducive to study.

On their visits to Sovereign Hill, today's children are discovering something of an often difficult past and also, perhaps, that present-day school is not so bad after all. The living history lessons that take them back 130 years have proved to be a valuable and unforgettable educational experiment for these children of Victoria.

BILLINUDGEL

Billinudgel comes slowly into focus out of the morning mist like some antipodean Brigadoon. If you chance upon it as you pass through the gentle green slopes of northcoast New South Wales, you will be enchanted, but beware—Billinudgel could well be the end of your road.

The legendary Brigadoon is said to appear in Scotland once every hundred years—for just one day. If you stay there as the evening mist swirls back in, you will stay forever. The same, it seems, is true of Billinudgel. The little town does not wrap visitors in the mist and dissolve with them, but it does capture and hold them with a strange magnetic attraction.

Margaret Alice Ring was not the first to fall under the spell, but her name became synonymous with the legend. 'I had no intentions of buying this place or coming here at all,' said Margaret Alice. 'This place' was the local hotel. Margaret Alice was passing through what was a timber town in the 1920s, on her way to a prospective hotel purchase in the nearby town of Casino.

She enjoyed a drink and a chat with the Billinudgel publican, and dropped in again on the way home. It was late, so Margaret Alice decided to stay overnight.

Margaret Alice was enchanted by a gypsy woman who said, 'Listen. Don't ever leave here. You will be as happy a person as ever you could be.'

More than fifty years later, Margaret Alice was still in Billinudgel, her initials over the pub making her known affectionately as 'Ma' Ring.

Ma Ring died at the age of 101. Until the day she died she tended the bar and held court over lively daily sessions of euchre. At any time her companions at the card table could include an accountant, a soldier, a teacher or a panel beater. They seem an unlikely selection of candidates for enchantment, but Billinudgel casts poetic spells.

Consider Colonel Bill Sorsby, the military man from Canberra's corridors of power. He abandoned the nation's capital for a pig farm at Billinudgel. He smiles as

GHITA FIORELLI

The small northern New South Wales town of Billinudgel—an Aboriginal name for the king parrot. The town has a reputation for seducing and capturing visitors. Many of the visitors to Billinudgel intend to pass through, but are drawn to stay by the town's indefinable magic.

GHITA FIORELLI

The Billinudgel hotel is named after Margaret Alice Ring, who was passing through the town in the 1920s and, like many others, never left. Ma Ring ran the bar and presided over the pub's euchre table until she died at the age of 101, and in doing so she fulfilled the prophesy of an old gypsy who told her she should never leave Billinudgel.

he compares the pig pens with his former headquarters, but he is serious about his charges. His prize pig is named Byron. Byron's predecessors were Shelley, Keats and Milton, and Colonel Sorsby has plans to introduce Longfellow as Byron's replacement.

Another visitor to Billinudgel, Ernie Kemp, booked into Ma's hotel for a holiday. Somehow, he just could not bring himself to book out. He stayed on as 'honorary gardener'.

Billinudgel, the 'new Brigadoon' lurking in misty ambush, is anything but a retirement village. Ma Ring was middle-aged when her horse-drawn carriage stopped on a dirt track outside a strangely appealing hotel. The many who followed were young and successful city folk who brought their children, whose children in turn were to be born among the enchanted hills. They are still coming. The little schoolhouse is alive with the sound of young merriment, which gives way to the more serious work of helping out after school on the tiny family properties that dot the hillsides. Retired teacher Spencer Jones says, 'Very little has changed in the town.'

When the day's work is done, they still gather at the New Brighton Hotel—Ma Ring's. It is the social centre of Billinudgel, with Ma's successors keeping her traditions, and the euchre table recalling her long dominance, her jolly laugh, her grinning triumphs.

Ma delighted in telling and retelling the words of that old gypsy woman who exhorted her to stay. She told Ma one more thing: 'Never sell the hotel, or you will die.' Margaret Alice Ring never did sell, and when she died at·101, she probably felt it was a fair deal.

If you chance upon the New Brighton Hotel one afternoon, do not linger. The sound of a shirtless young farm worker playing a haunting tune on the old upright piano may just hold you until the evening mist closes over Billinudgel—and you.

Harry Addison ran a panel beating business in Sydney. He thought that there must be a better way of earning a living. Harry was not an unwary traveller snared during passage, but was lured by an invitation from friends to visit them. That was all he needed. The panel beater who had never been on a horse in his life bought a cattle farm, rides with the best of Billinudgel,

GHITA FIORELLI

GHITA FIORELLI

The hotel is the town's social centre and the spot where locals gather after work; or where unsuspecting travellers stop for a beer on the verandah. Although the legendary Ma Ring is no longer there, the long tradition of hospitality is upheld at the old weatherboard hotel.

and has only been back to Sydney once. 'I could not get out of Sydney fast enough,' he said.

What is it, then, about the magic village whose name means nothing to most Australians? The first settlers were timber-getters, and when the timber ran out, they planted bananas. It was green, gently rolling land with rich soil favoured by a generous climate. However, there were two forces stronger than the power of Billinudgel—an economy that drove prices down, and crop disease that wiped out plantations and sent growers back unwillingly to the cities.

Billinudgel is the name Aborigines gave the king parrot. One day, all the billinudgels flew away, never to return. That was the last mass exodus. Slowly, people began being drawn back, and like Ma Ring, drawn in. The canyons of commerce relinquished city accountant Tony Berry. On the banana-green slopes of Billinudgel, he and partner Alan Barker harvested bunches of bananas weighing more than 50 kilograms.

At first, the magic was missing. Tony Berry recalled that when he first started the plantation he thought it would kill him. 'At the end of the day I was not fit for very much at all.' Tony's fitness improved, the plantation was successful enough to keep his and Alan's families— and to take him back into commerce, but only as far as the village. He runs a new supermarket.

Spencer Jones reflects, 'I probably have let opportunities go.' He came to Billinudgel as a schoolteacher, and certainly had no plans to stay. His first pleasant surprise, after simply absorbing the beauty of the area, was a working bee of the locals. They descended on him, clearing up the schoolyard and providing gym equipment. Billinudgel was weaving its spell around him. 'After weighing up the pros and cons, and after weighing up the family situation, I decided that I did not think we could have done much better,' recalls Spencer. He still has not found anything better, having stayed with the little Billinudgel schoolhouse, and retired without regrets for any lost opportunities.

There are those who will do just about anything to stay. Bob Spring, a baker by trade, has worked in the wheat belt and on sheep stations, built a prawn trawler and worked on it, and then took up road construction around Billinudgel, 'just to stay in the area.'

SUNSHINE MAN

Rows of Sunshine Harvesters await despatch from Hugh McKay's factory.

WELDON TRANNIES

One beautiful January day in Bendigo in 1883, the McKay brothers, John and Hugh, were hard at work on their family farm. Though generally cheerful about their duties around the property, on this particular day they were in the middle of their most dreaded task. Winnowing—separating the chaff from the grain by hand—was a rotten job, considered to be too cruel a task for horses and, in their dislike of this work, the brothers were not alone. However, an Australian invention was about to revolutionise farming and agriculture throughout the world and Hugh McKay was to be its inventor.

Hugh McKay was only seventeen years old in 1883, but he was inventive and determined to do away with the unpopular task of hand winnowing. Hugh believed that he could build a machine, something like the stripping equipment that had been in use for thirty years, to clean grain. He was not the first to think of this. Many had tried, but so far no one had found the mechanism to

make the machine work dependably and efficiently. Undaunted, Hugh persuaded his father to let him try his hand at invention. With brother John, he built a timber blacksmith's shop on the farm, and they salvaged every piece of machinery they could find. The boys worked right through the winter of 1883 and into the following summer, toiling on their invention whenever possible.

The harvester took them almost a year to design, build and modify, and by February 1884 the brothers were ready to test it out on one hectare of grain fields. Miraculously, the machine worked, and at the end of the trial run, Hugh could proudly hold up a handful of clean grain. His idea had become a reality. He might have been young but, before long, Hugh had patented his invention and built five more machines along the same lines as the prototype. The problem then was to sell his machines. In the beginning it was not easy; many farmers had already spent a great deal of money on farm machinery while others were sceptical of the new idea.

Australian Broadcasting Corporation

Australian Broadcasting Corporation

Above and top. *Before Hugh McKay and his brother John invented the Sunshine Harvester, the difficult task of winnowing (as shown in this reconstruction) had to be done by hand. The McKay brothers' inventiveness paid off, and in 1884 their harvester was in operation.*

One farmer even believed that God intended winnowing to be hard work, and that it was a sin to make it easier. Nevertheless, Hugh was persuasive; buyers began to appear and before too long his five machines had been purchased. The agricultural revolution had found its first recruits.

Farmers became aware that the machine could save 80 per cent of their harvesting costs and its popularity boomed. Hugh opened a factory in Ballarat and named the machine the Sunshine Harvester, inspired by a term 'sunshine of God' that he had heard at a prayer meeting. Despite its early success, the venture ran into financial difficulties. In 1892, Hugh was bankrupt but, by borrowing money from friends and making a determined effort, he was able to buy his company back.

The tide had turned for the Sunshine Harvester, and by the end of the century the enterprising farm boy had become one of the country's leading industrialists. Even during the great drought of 1901, Hugh profited by making a bold move; he shipped 50 harvesters to Argentina, accompanied by his brother Sam, and though they did not sell in South America, wheat growers from the United States were impressed and bought every machine. By 1904 Hugh's business was thriving. By exporting an incredible 25,000 harvesters to 14 countries, Hugh McKay had become the first major industrial exporter in Australia's history.

Following his success, pirate copies of his harvester were being made in the United States and sold in Australia, so in 1907 Hugh requested government protection. His appeal before the new arbitration court became an historic test case, known as the *Harvester Judgment*, that did much to change the industrial scene. Hugh was told that if he could prove that his workers received a fair and decent wage, he would receive tariff protection. Hugh had always believed that no employee deserved to be paid more than he was worth, and worked on the principle of paying his men in proportion to the amount they contributed to the finished product. The court, under Mr Justice Higgins, did not agree and ruled that seven shillings a day was an appropriate wage for all of Hugh's workers. It was an interesting decision because until this time employers had been free to decide what they should pay their workers. But this was a new era—the beginning of the notion of a basic wage.

Hugh McKay received his tariff protection but he was not happy with the wage decision. However, Edward Russell, the secretary of the Agricultural Implement

The Sunshine Header Harvester revolutionised Australian farming at the end of the last century. The farmers' initial scepticism was overcome by the machine's undoubted efficiency.

WELDON TRANNIES

Despite a shaky start, the McKay business thrived, and by 1904 the ex-farm boy had become Australia's first major industrial exporter.

Makers' Union, was delighted. He rightly believed that this test case would ensure that eventually every industrial worker would receive, under a national award system, a decent minimum wage. It was what his and other unions had been striving for over many years.

This was not the end of Hugh's troubles, and Edward Russell was to become the thorn in the side of the McKay business. By the beginning of 1910, the union had grown considerably, and most of Hugh's workers were members, leaving only a few who could not be persuaded to join. The union was demanding compulsory unionism and Hugh persistently fought what he considered to be interference in his business: he was asked to force all his employees to join the union, or sack them if they refused. The explosive situation culminated in a strike and the factory temporarily ceased operating. But, as is the case in many strikes, it was ultimately the workers who suffered more than the employer. After three months of stalemate, the men returned to work, and McKay had lost only a small percentage of his annual production. The union had lost its bid for compulsory membership.

By the 1920s, McKay's business was thriving to the extent that almost every piece of farm machinery in Australia was being made at his factory which employed 3,000 workers and covered an area of 12 hectares. The McKay family had become wealthy and had reached the zenith of Australian society. At their property near Melbourne, they entertained distinguished visitors, such as prime ministers Billy Hughes and Stanley Bruce, who often came to ask Hugh's advice on agricultural policies. Young Hughie, the farm boy, had come a long way, but by 1926 he was was stricken with cancer. Despite treatment by London doctors, Hugh returned home to die when he was only sixty-one years old.

After Hugh's death, the McKay business continued until 1955 when the giant Canadian multi-national company Massey Ferguson took over the business. With the takeover, no trace remained of the inspired Australian farm boy whose invention had revolutionised farming the world over. Today, few Australians know of Hugh Victor McKay or the 'Sunshine Man'.

THE WOMEN

Green and black are the colours of the seasons. That is how the outback schoolboy draws them, and his teacher, in a town far away, is puzzled by this concept.

The teacher, charged with the responsibility of educating the boy by correspondence lessons, has something to learn from the outback student. Where he lives, there is the Wet, mantling the sere landscape in green. Then there is the burn-off, and the land is blackened—the boy's 'seasons' are green and black.

Australia's correspondence system has helped many isolated families cope with the need for education, but the vast distances between teacher and student can demonstrate differences in perception. The teacher is inculcated with the idea of four seasons; the outback child knows only what he sees.

Colleen and Frank Sims discovered these differences in perception as they travelled throughout far north Queensland. The Sims were itinerant teachers, making twice-yearly treks over thousands of square kilometres, visiting Australia's most isolated children.

Early this century their predecessors travelled on horseback or horse-and-buggy. When Colleen and Frank took up the trail a couple of decades later, they had a four-wheel-drive vehicle, but the days of bumping over often vestigial tracks were only slightly less arduous. The earlier itinerants used to stay on a station for a week, and and children were brought in from other areas. The new 'gypsy teachers' sometimes stayed only overnight, but their visits were vital.

Molly lives in the isolated outback. She is one parent who is grateful for the Sims' dedication. With her husband away for much of the year, Molly boils up her laundry in a wood-fired copper in a bare clearing ringed by silent gum trees. She irons with a petrol-powered iron, whose dull roar is replaced at night by the hiss of a pressured oil lamp. With no electricity, Molly and her son bend their heads close to the pages of the correspondence lessons.

Molly felt intimidated by her role as teacher, having little confidence in her own ability to guide her son and answer his questions. Then Frank and Colleen arrived and found that Molly's son had a slight learning disability. By recognising it, the teachers gave the boy a better chance, and Molly gained renewed confidence to carry out the vital task of supervising daily schoolwork. 'I think Molly and women like her are really great,' says Colleen, 'I just could not cope with that loneliness.'

There are about 150 children on properties scattered across the far north of Queensland. Some of them have problems they would never encounter if they were not so isolated.

On one small property, a Dutch-born former social worker and his Swiss-born wife, a former draughts-

WELDON TRANNIES

Isolated outback families are aware of the need to give their children a proper education. Educational facilities vary from correspondence course papers to sophisticated computer equipment.

woman and artist, had to overcome additional obstacles. They moved to the Outback for a freer life but their English was still poor. They had to learn to speak English well before they could teach their children and help them with their correspondence lessons. Itinerant teachers were a major boost to their efforts.

On these properties, big or small, there is always work to be done. Yet the parents realise the importance of education and sometimes everything stops in order to make time for the children's lessons. At Bagstowe Station, Tom and Mary Dixon are kept busy managing their beef cattle. At home, Mary cooks for everyone. When the cattle have to be mustered, she joins the family and other stockmen on horseback, usually for three or four weeks of camping, cooking and mustering. At night, there are still the correspondence school papers to be read.

Outback children concentrate on their school work. Mothers bear the brunt of the responsibility for their children's education, and welcome the moral support provided by visits from itinerant teachers.

Mary's daughter has the advantage of a School of the Air radio, but that does not make her lessons easier. The muster comes to a halt; a Landrover is hooked up to provide radio power; an aerial wire snakes up through the gumtree branches; and Mary's daughter sits at a portable table in the middle of the sun-bleached bush, and after listening carefully to the faraway voice of her teacher through the static replies solemnly: 'Good morning, Miss—Over.'

Mary says, 'I think—well, I hope—that I am giving them enough background to carry on so that when they go to boarding school they should be on an equal footing with children who have been to ordinary school.'

Mary Dixon even tried employing a full-time teacher, a governess, but it was not successful. The governess was unpopular. Mary says that 'she ended up doing the housework and I was doing her job.' That seemed expensive and pointless and the governess left. About a year later Colleen and Frank Sims came along to provide help and encourage confidence in Mary to supervise her children's education.

Technology — computers, radios, satellites — has helped much of the world overcome the tyranny of distance, but this area of Australia has special needs. The distances are great, the number of people populating it is minimal. The system that worked well nearly a century ago is still proving its practicality as we approach the twenty-first century.

After ten years of dust, heat, floods, bumps and bogs, Frank and Colleen Sims abandoned their itinerant lifestyle. In Cairns, Frank became co-ordinator of the Priority Country Area Programme while Colleen took up a position as co-ordinator of a career training course at a private secondary school helping the country boys assimilate into the city and encouraging the city boys to enjoy the country. Nevertheless, Frank says he cannot see an end to the itinerant teaching program. In fact, he and Colleen were replaced by two couples. They both miss the people who welcomed them for what they brought, not only in morale-boosting assistance but a greater mutual understanding between town teachers and bush folk.

People like Molly and Mary may live without electricity and telephones, and their children may think that the idea of four distinct seasons is mere theory, but Colleen is not at all sure that they are disadvantaged. 'They learn so much of real life by being out in a mustering camp. Most of them are going to work on properties and their education is appropriate to their lifestyle. They are getting the best of "both worlds".'

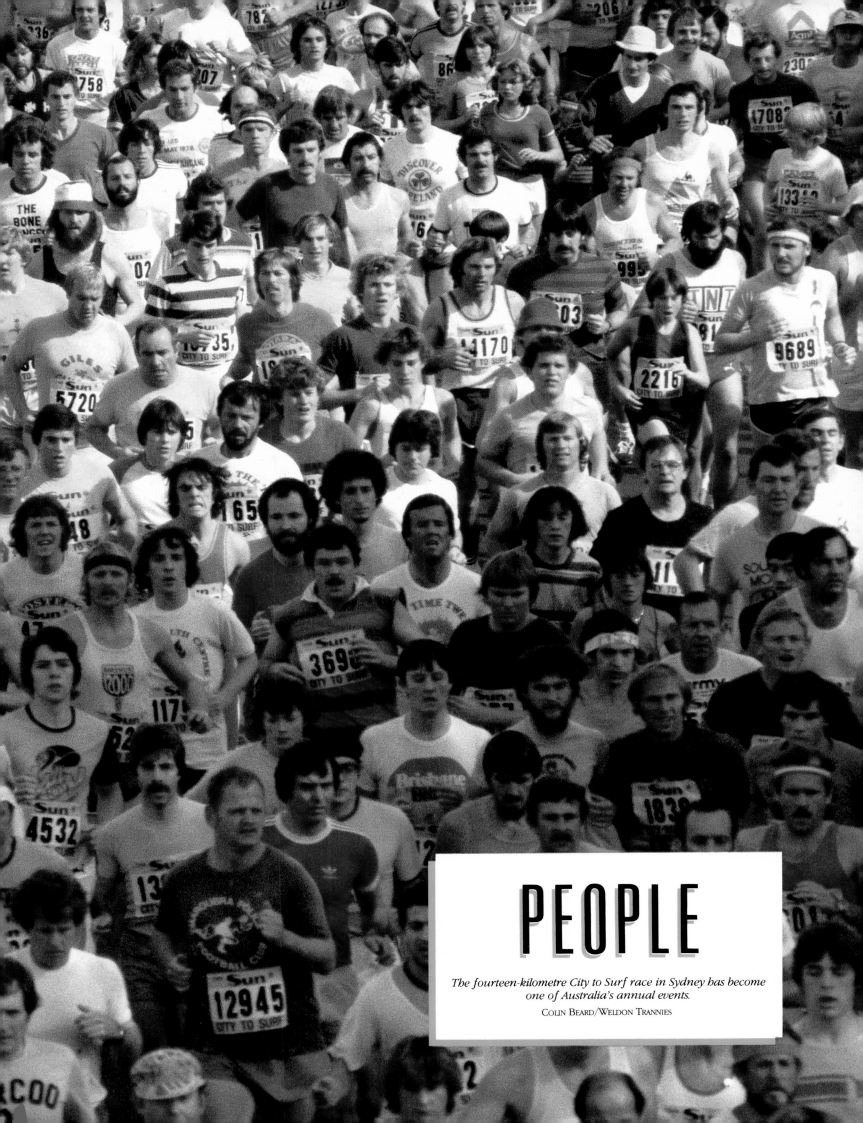

PEOPLE

The fourteen-kilometre City to Surf race in Sydney has become one of Australia's annual events.

COLIN BEARD/WELDON TRANNIES

SHE SIMPLY WANTED TO FLY

Her name was Bird, but they called her the Flying Angel. Either way, she was certainly a flier. She first took to the air with one of the world's best aviators, Sir Charles Kingsford Smith.

The famous 'Smithy' took Nancy-Bird Walton as his first pupil in 1933, when Sydney's international airport comprised half a dozen crude buildings, a grassy paddock and planes made from wood, wire and cloth.

Nancy was only thirteen when she was bitten by the flying bug. She was serious about it and saved every penny she could. Three years later, Smithy accepted her into his fledgling Kingsford Smith Flying School. She flew every day, picking up as many skills as she could, including engineering. 'I realised', she said, 'that if I came down somewhere, I would have to get myself back in the air.'

After doing figure eights around the Sydney aerodrome shed for her licence test, she won her wings. Nevertheless, it was hard to make people believe that she had become a professional pilot. Luckily, Nancy's great-aunt decided to help. She had planned to leave Nancy two hundred pounds in her will, but said that she would give it to Nancy immediately if her father would equal the amount. He did, and Nancy, armed with four hundred pounds, shopped around for a plane she could afford. She found one in the guise of Gypsy Moth VH-UTN. It was not in the best condition, but Nancy had enthusiasm and, together with the rebuilding team, the Gypsy Moth was made airworthy.

During this time, Nancy racked her brains for an inspiration as to what she was going to do with the Gypsy Moth. By 1934, barnstorming (taking people for

Above and opposite. Nancy-Bird Walton began her flying career in 1933 and set a shining example for aspiring female aviators.

joy flights) was really a thing of the past, but that is what Nancy chose. She 'dreamed of making a fortune.' Another woman pilot, Peggy McKillop, agreed to join her, although, as Nancy admits, 'We were told we could not hope to make a go of it. But what else could we do?'

They flew low over country towns to gain people's attention, then landed and began their sales pitch — 'Would anybody like to come up with me? It is only ten shillings a ticket.' While some accepted the invitation to see their properties from above, others declined. 'Some smart alecks would buy tickets for their friends and persuade them to go up,' recalled Nancy. She would provide unadvertised thrills with some hair-raising dives and spins.

Nancy made enough money from barnstorming to keep the Gypsy Moth in reasonable repair, but a visit to Bourke, New South Wales, led Nancy to engage in flying for a different purpose. While at Bourke, she was asked to take a country clinic Sister on one of her regular medical trips beyond the railhead. Shortly afterwards, Nancy and the Gypsy Moth became the first aerial ambulance service in New South Wales.

For people isolated west of the Darling River, Nancy was often the difference between life and death. She did not carry stretchers, but this did not prevent her from transporting some emergency cases. Admitting to some fear herself, she said: 'There were very few landmarks — the Darling River in the east, the border fence, one road slightly northwest, and another southwest. I was often afraid of being lost and not found till I had perished. Nobody really wants to die in isolation, slowly, beside a plane . . .'

The Great Air Race in 1936 caught her attention and she joined 30 other planes at a time when flying aids and air traffic control were almost non-existent. One of her fellow competitors was a young garage proprietor who had trouble scraping together the money to get his imported plane out of bond. He was Reg (later Sir Reginald) Ansett, who went on to establish one of Australia's major domestic airlines. Nancy did not win that race.

At about the same time, the regularly demanding and often harrowing aerial ambulance service work was beginning to be a strain on Nancy's nerves: 'I'd taken off for the west. I was tired, and so was my plane . . . I climbed towards the mountains, and the clouds were coming down. Everything in me revolted against going across the mountains.' She turned back. 'In my heart I knew it was the right decision, but I went home and cried. I had a "controlled breakdown".' Two years after

the big air race of 1936, Nancy-Bird Walton sold her plane and retired from flying.

The Second World War brought her back to flying. She served as a commandant of the Women's Air Training Corps until 1945. With two young children, Nancy did not think of flying again until 1949, but at that time she had trouble obtaining a licence. This did not concern her greatly until 1958 when she wanted to fly in a 'Powderpuff Derby' in the United States. 'I really did need a licence for that.'

In 1964, Reg Ansett, that young garage proprietor who had won the Great Air Race back in 1936, sponsored a major race from Brisbane to Adelaide. The race was the biggest gathering of light planes ever seen in Australia, and Nancy, flying a Victa, joined 145 other competitors. Again, Nancy did not win, but the sheer thrill of flying was invigorating.

In the 1980s, Nancy-Bird Walton was still flying a little, but as she explained 'My grandchildren are more important to me now.' However, she is proud of her achievement in being her state's first aerial ambulance. There was no such official service until thirty-three years later in 1967. She has fond memories of those wide-eyed country folk who paid for their friends to fly with her, then 'whispered in my ear to give them the works!'

With so many achievements, the Bird they called the Flying Angel of the outback still has some extraordinary regrets over opportunities missed: 'I did not fly over the early morning wildlife in Rhodesia, and I did not shoot the rapids in Japan!'

Right. Nancy-Bird Walton in more recent years. During the 1930s she made a living from flying her Gypsy Moth aircraft as the first aerial ambulance service in outback New South Wales. Later she served as Commandant of the Women's Air Training Corps during the Second World War.

TAIPAN MAN

The taipan (*Oxyuranus scutellatus*) is one of the world's deadliest and most aggressive snakes. Before the early 1950s, the risk of falling victim to its needle-like fangs did not seem great, for until that time it was believed that the taipan was confined to Australia's northeastern tip, Cape York Peninsula. It was found, however, that this was not the case.

Queensland snake expert Ram Chandra always believed the taipan could be found much further south, but nobody knew for certain until the early 1950s. Australia has 140 species of snakes, and at least twenty are dangerous; five or six are certain killers. Each year, about four snake-bite victims died in circumstances that baffled the paramedics working on these patients. In each case, they believed that the cause was a common brown snake bite, but they were not entirely sure.

The paramedics contacted Ram Chandra, who worked with the deadly taipan as part of his 'pit of death' snake act. He was certain that the authorities were wrong about the taipan's habitat.

Ram milked his serpents in an attempt to collect enough venom so that an antivenene could be developed. The first successful antivenene was produced in 1955 and was made available to Ram who was at constant risk of being bitten while performing with his taipans.

The needled fangs of the taipan are 12 millimetres long, and one squirt into a milking bottle produces 150 milligrams. There is one report of a single taipan sending a 300 milligram jet into the safety of a jar. Taipan venom contains three threatening ingredients: neurotoxin, which causes paralysis, loss of vision and hearing; a haemolysin, which virtually turns the blood to water; and a coagulant, which clots the blood. Death usually follows about three hours after a bite.

Although other snake bites had affected the use of his legs, before early 1956 Ram Chandra had not been bitten by a taipan. He was nevertheless determined to help find an antivenene because he was convinced that the taipan lurked much further south and was therefore

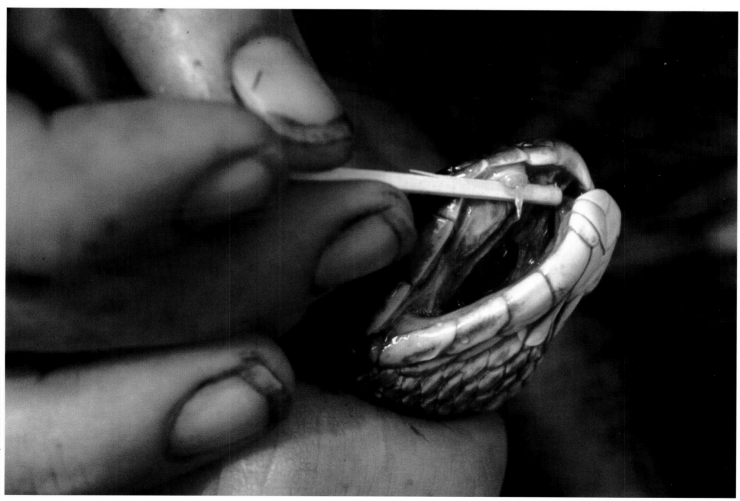

D. STAMMER/AUSTRALIAN MUSEUM

*The taipan (*Oxyuranus scutellatus*), one of the world's deadliest snakes, injects its victim with venom from its fangs*

Above. *Ram Chandra, the Queensland taipan expert, who has worked with the venomous creatures for many years. Ram milked his snakes of their poison in order to produce an antivenene which could save many lives.*

Left. *The lethal, brown-coloured, 2-metre-long taipan is Australia's most feared snake, and the most aggressive of the continent's 130 species. Despite theories to the contrary, Ram believed that the taipan did not inhabit just the Cape York Peninsula, but also lived much further south. His opinion was confirmed when a young schoolboy was bitten by a taipan in Cairns.*

more of a threat than was believed. Time proved Ram to be right.

In 1955, an eleven-year-old schoolboy, Bruce Stringer, was struck during morning recess, on the edge of the schoolgrounds in Cairns. His description of the snake fitted that of a taipan. Bruce lay critically ill for fourteen hours while doctors administered a commonly used antivenene. Bruce's condition grew worse, but the doctors could not imagine that a taipan would be so far south from the Peninsula. As a last resort, it was decided to try the new antivenene. Within a couple of hours, the symptoms faded. Ram said: 'I'd risked my life all those years and now it seemed that all my dreams had come true because the child had lived.' To show his gratitude, Bruce Stringer became a medical doctor.

A couple of months after the incident with Bruce, Ram was bitten by a taipan. His persistence in convincing the authorities of the need for a taipan antivenene had paid off. He became the second person to survive a taipan bite through the use of the antivenene.

NEW ACHIEVEMENTS

In two hundred years of European settlement, Australia's Aborigines have been given few opportunities to participate in a frequently alien European world. All too often ignored, Aborigines were relegated to the fringes of society and given little responsibility for their own future and destiny. Even when employed as a jackaroo or stockman on a cattle station, the Aborigine's role was always one of assistance, rather than a position of command and control.

In the Northern Territory, at last the situation is changing. The Territory's land rights laws of 1976 have given Aborigines a greater command of their own land, and changing attitudes have given them unprecedented opportunities in many fields of employment. A new era has dawned where Aborigines' capabilities and the contribution that they can make to both European and Aboriginal society are recognised.

Ian Goombala is a teacher. He graduated from college and now teaches Aboriginal children, mostly in their own language. This is an achievement in itself because European Australians have long frowned upon communication in native tongues. Now it is the basis of a special education system that has achieved great success. As a representative of the Darwin Aboriginal community explained, the value of the new scheme's policy of teaching in native languages is that Aborigines who have not been able to succeed in the European education system now can go back to their communities and manage their affairs because they have been educated in a manner that is meaningful to them.

Young people are also being instructed in the field of health and medicine. The Department of Health training course is designed to train and then send Aborigines back to their communities with the medical knowledge necessary to make a contribution to their people. At Alice Springs, for example, the Central Australian Aboriginal Congress provides a service that employs both modern health care and traditional bush medicine. The clinic is run and staffed totally by Aborigines, who converse with the patients in their Aboriginal tongue. As a result, the patients feel more comfortable in the clinic than in what seems to them the alien atmosphere of the Alice Springs· hospital. In the clinic, they have a sense of belonging.

There are many other fields in which Aborigines are now serving their community. Albert Japandawa is a police aide playing an important role in liaising between Aborigines and authorities in the preservation of law and order. Being able to communicate with the Aborigines in their own dialects and knowing tribal customs and social behaviour give Albert a tremendous advantage over a white police officer. It is an obvious concept and works well. The only surprising thing about it is that the authorities have taken so long to initiate the police aide program.

Northern Territory Aborigines are also being trained in the fields of commerce and business enterprise. Success in these areas will give their communities important financial independence as well as the self-esteem that accompanies responsibility. Women in one community have turned to their sewing machines to make clothing, including many of Darwin's school uniforms. Another group near Katherine has set up a

Aboriginal children at Yuendemu, in the Northern Territory.

Opposite:
Top. *A small community school in Kakadu,*
Northern Territory, caters for the local children.
Bottom. *One of Australia's most accomplished Aboriginal artists,*
Jeffrey Samuels, completing a major work.

CLAUDE COIRAULT

WELDON TRANNIES

LEO MEIER/WELDON TRANNIES

much larger and more ambitious project. Baruwei Enterprises was established by the local Aboriginal community to form a wholesale food supply service for the shops in the area. It has been a resounding success, increasing the volume of sales to include everything from pencils to bicycles. Their turnover is more than $100,000 a year.

Another example of this policy is demonstrated in a co-operative supermarket scheme. Men and women are trained in all aspects of the retail trade, with an emphasis on self-management that is working well in many parts of the Territory. These enterprises ensure that the profits are kept and utilised within the community.

Aboriginal art is gaining recognition and approval throughout Australia and overseas. Communities like the Tiwi people, on a remote island north of Darwin, are benefiting from the increased wealth that their traditional arts have brought them. The beautiful Tiwi pottery, silk-screened fabrics, crafts and paintings are sold through the local arts and craft sales agent and flown off the island to art galleries and shops both in Australia and overseas. It is not only the art of the Tiwi people that deserves praise, but also the success of their self-run business enterprise.

Aboriginal people have always known and understood their land, and it is appropriate that the new era of responsibility has seen Aborigines initiating their own farming and pastoral projects, both small and large. Near Katherine, a small patch of wild bush has been cleared, irrigated and planted with vegetables to create a model farm that has set the pattern for many others in the Territory. At the other end of the scale, vast cattle stations are now under the control of Aborigines who once worked only in the supporting roles of mustering, droving and horse-breaking. Australia's original bushmen are proving that their unique understanding of the land can lead to success in raising stock, as well as running a large business.

For Nelson Mullaring, a ranger with Northern Territory's Conservation Commission, the new policy has created a role that he considers symbolic. In his job Nelson supplies ranger stations, eradicates pests such as wild pigs, and keeps a close watch on the numbers of tourists that visit the wildlife sanctuaries. He is a modern guardian of the land that his ancestors walked for thousands of years. It may be a new era of achievement but, for Nelson, such a job enables him to fulfil the rightful and traditional obligation that he has inherited from his forefathers.

Left. Aboriginal art has become immensely popular, not just in Australia, but overseas also. Galleries such as this sell paintings, pottery, carvings, fabrics and basketwork. High prices are now being paid for such works, and most of the profits are returned to the artists and their communities.

SURF SHAPER

Every dedicated surfboard rider has the same dream: perfect waves on an empty beach. Yet even with a vast coastline our most fanatical surfers still find on seemingly empty beaches the footprints and see the bobbing heads of riders who are already there. Today, there are so many board riders in Australia that a whole generation of new surfers probably believe that the sport has always existed.

One such dedicated wave-seeker remembers distinctly the time when it seemed that the whole world took to the water on surfboards. Bob McTavish eyes the beaches with a mixture of pride and regret: regret because empty beaches are a dream of the past and pride because he is the man who filled them.

Bob McTavish invented what is known as the short board. By making boards lighter, and approximately one metre shorter, the future of surfing was reshaped. Anyone could now lift and carry a surfboard; it was easier to learn to ride it; and, at last, surfing was no longer simply a matter of standing on a long, heavy 'Malibu' board and heading straight across the wave. For the first time, riders could carve up and down the face of a wave.

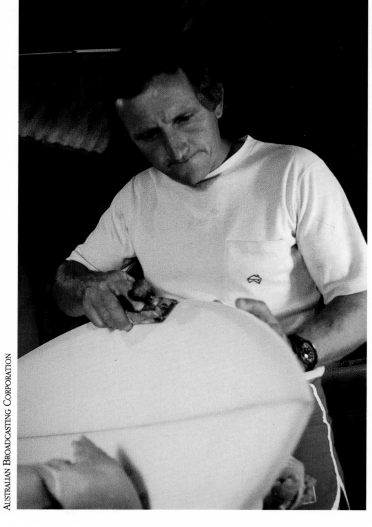

AUSTRALIAN BROADCASTING CORPORATION

AUSTRALIAN BROADCASTING CORPORATION

Most of the young surfers who accept short boards as a way of life would not recognise Bob McTavish as anything more than a slightly balding 'wrinkly' who seems to be having a bit of fun on the smaller waves. In fact Bob loves surfing the smaller waves with his family. 'I find a lot of fun in surfing the little waves which people pass by. They don't care about those waves because they're not as big, long, green and glossy as the magazines and surf films have led them to expect. However, they're still waves to me and it is still fun to get out in the water.'

Top. *Bob McTavish, the man who invented the short board. He reshaped the old, cumbersome 'Malibu', and in the process filled the seas with surfing devotees who were inspired by the new lightweight board, and its manoeuvrability.*
Left. *Bob McTavish has always enjoyed surfing which has become both his sport and occupation.*

Opposite. *British surfer Martin Potter is known for his ability to manoeuvre the short board.*
Overleaf. *Greg Tulau shaving everything off the top of a wave.*
TIM STORER

Fun is what Bob often talks about. He calls himself the 'original surf rat'. In the 1960s he lived only to chase the waves. Those revolutionary times, he says, were bedevilled by government corruption, the Cuban missile crisis, and the constant threat of a nuclear holocaust. 'We dreaded thinking about the future. There did not seem to be one.' With his friends George Greenough and Chris Brock, Bob lived the life of a wild young man— riding around in old cars and living in shacks with little idea of working, other than shaping boards. Surfing provided an escape from the real world.

Sitting on boards and around campfires, Bob and his friends talked endlessly about surfing and how it could be improved. This idle speculation gave birth to the short board: Bob was the first to reduce the weight of a board to 4.5 kilograms (10 pounds) by cutting 60–90 centimetres (2–3 feet) off the average board lengths.

Inexorably the 'original' surf rat was drawn back into the world he had spurned — and a future. Instead of sleeping in old cars, Bob settled with his wife and family in a self-designed home on the balmy coast of New South Wales and began a small surfboard business. Faced with a growing family and a new sense of responsibility, the surfing dropout became a businessman.

He built and sold his short boards, always working on modifications. It could take 20 to 30 experimental boards a year before a particular combination proved successful. The key to success was to find the areas where the board did not respond to the potential of the wave.

According to Bob, the wave is the most important element in surfing, closely followed by the shape of the board. 'The craftsmanship could be compared to, perhaps, making a musical instrument, like a guitar or a violin. They might all look alike to the inexperienced eye, until you pick them up and play them. A surfboard is much the same. Each one is handmade, its quality depending on how well it is played.'

With his wife and family, Bob continues to surf the smaller waves and, when the beach is not crowded, occasionally ventures out to ride the big waves.

One group of young surfers who definitely appreciate the knowledge of this 'tribal elder' is the Byron Seahorses Boardriding Club. The 'zinc and boardies' set cram the club shed to learn from the 'master'. Bob says that to surf well one must adopt a set of rules, governed and dominated by gymnastic manoeuvres. The young audience knows Bob McTavish as a man with many surfing titles to his credit. They enjoy hearing his thoughts on surfing. The fun-chasing dropout who became a successful businessman with a family has a unique perspective on the sport of surfing: more sheer fun in the waves for more people.

Right. *The ultimate experience — staying in the tube.*

Tim Storer

THE BEAR

ANDREW ROBERTS

Vicki Roycroft is a born winner but her horse, The Bear, was a loser from the day he was born. At least that is what everyone told Vicki when the leading Australian equestrienne first saw a stunted five-year-old horse with a funny name. The Bear won her heart.

People who had a good knowledge of horses told Vicki that the animal was too small to be a jumper, but she saw in him a potential showjumping champion, and she was determined to prove it. Vicki believed The Bear had a big heart that could overcome his small stature, and if anyone knew about big hearts, it was Vicki. She had come to riding relatively late, at the age of twelve. By the time this city girl was fifteen, she was winning on the Australian showjumping circuit. She continued to do so and after marrying Wayne Roycroft, a former Australian showjumping champion, she went on to win even bigger titles. Wayne's father, Bill, had been the country's most celebrated rider with five Olympic games to his credit.

Wayne and Vicki lived and worked together on their property just north of Sydney, bringing thoroughbred yearlings to the racing circuit. Wayne became Vicki's coach. He believes that championship showjumping needs complete communication between horse and rider. 'It is something every rider tries for, but few achieve.' With The Bear, he agrees that Vicki achieved it — a perfect relationship. Vicki agrees: 'If he were a person, he'd be my best friend.'

The couple worked with The Bear, aiming to overcome his smallness by taking advantage of their special relationship with him, and the big heart that drove The Bear to try harder, never holding back as the height of a fence increased. The Bear had another advantage, a natural spring. He would lose that as he grew older, but Vicki was determined to take him through the major showjumping titles as he approached his peak. Her biggest dream was to ride The Bear in the Los Angeles Olympics.

Working towards that goal, they went on the road around Australia. The horse fanciers who had shaken their heads at the presumption of the runt with the funny name cheered as the pair scored victories over former Olympic showjumpers and national champions. The Bear, together with Vicki, qualified for the Olympics and was the only Australian horse to jump clear in both the cross-country and showjumping sections of the gruelling Olympic Three Day Event.

The Bear carried Vicki over the first hurdles to great

ANDREW ROBERTS

victories. In 1987, she competed on the European jumping circuit. Showjumping is a major and highly-respected sport throughout Europe, with live and television audiences giving it the kind of attention that Australians give to football. Vicki's European titles were capped by a rare achievement when she won the Grand Prix of Rome, the first Australian and the first woman ever to do so.

The Bear is now happy in retirement on the Roycroft's Mount White property, north of Sydney. Vicki's showjumping achievements have not stopped there, but nevertheless they began with a little horse that everyone said would never be a jumper.

ANDREW ROBERTS

Above. *Despite The Bear's small size, Vicki's patient training, along with the horse's great natural character and determination, turned him into a champion.*
Right. *Vicki and The Bear have always had a very special relationship — the perfect ingredient for championship show jumping.*

Opposite. *Top Australian showjumper, Vicki Roycroft and her horse, The Bear, take one of the hundreds of jumps they have tackled together. This winning team has won many titles, including the coveted Grand Prix of Rome.*

BOGONG HIGH PLAINS

The tough men who live in the Australian Alps, in the wild and remote area they call the Bogong High Plains, did not take kindly to a slim young Norwegian, especially when he started asking questions about their way of life. 'Bloody city slicker. What the hell does he know about horses and high plains?' Tor Holth recalls their comment with amusement and understanding.

These days he is greeted with 'Hi Tor. How are you going?' It is a measure of his success among the locals, who no longer consider him just a 'city slicker' artist and writer who started riding and walking in their country, the high plains that makes up 2,500 square kilometres of southeastern Australia.

Tor won acceptance by treating the local people with respect and sensitivity, as well as by sheer persistence. He recalls once riding in a blizzard and the terror of a complete whiteout. 'I could not see the pommel of my saddle. After an interminable period, I reached Towonga Hut but I was so frozen I had to be helped out of the saddle.'

Tor first came to the mountains and the High Plains to paint. Born in China of missionary parents, he trained as an architect, though his background also included working as an equestrian instructor, folk singer, author and artist. He said, 'I thought it would be easy to paint the Bogong High Plains but I found they had moods which could not be tamed. So, I had to adapt myself and my style to that of the mountains; I had to change my familiar colours from Europe to a new range in Australia. But, I found a great love for these High Plains and their solitude. Unlike Europe, one can walk for days and not meet a soul.'

Much of the vast area is inaccessible by car. Finding it impossible to personally carry enough supplies for the time required, Tor used packhorses with loads of about 250 kilograms, enough to sustain him for three or four weeks, through both good weather and the deadly blinding snowstorms that can quickly strike. Using maps and following clear trails, Tor soon knew the wilderness like the best of the mountain men.

Though his first plan was to paint a series of paintings of the High Plains, Tor discovered the rude huts that dotted the area and wanted to know more about the people who had built them. The huts were used by cattlemen who grazed their stock and mustered them in the autumn. They lived alone, surrounded by the beauty and the danger of the mountains. Tor described the huts as the cosiest of places, especially when the wind was howling outside and the snow was blowing in horizontally through some of the cracks in the walls. 'Imagine a roaring fire in there and a camp oven sizzling away, a billy of tea standing by. You might even have a glass of claret . . .!'

AUSTRALIAN BROADCASTING COMMISSION

The tough and independent men of the Bogong High Plains were wary of Tor Holth but eventually accepted him as their friend.
Opposite: *Riders make their way along the ridges of the Bogong High Plains.*

The hut people he wanted to learn about ignored him at first, but then slowly became drawn to the city feller with the foreign accent. After a few years and nearly 5000 kilometres of riding and walking a criss-cross trail over the plains, he had won their friendship and respect. At times he was broke, not knowing where his next money was coming from, but still he found he could not stop. Tor shared the cattlemen's huts when the weather worsened and found that he not only wanted to paint, but also to write about his new friends — to preserve a way of life and to honour these men.

During his first years of research, he married Jane, a book editor. Their mutual love of the high country convinced them to give up their jobs in the city to travel in the High Plains and write books about this remote area and the cattlemen who live there. The couple delight in the country, especially when Mount Feathertop is teased by clouds gathering over a ridge dusted with late snow. As they both relax around a campfire to listen to master yarn-spinners like Mick Walsh tell true tales about these plains, Tor says Mick can talk all night and day without repeating a single story. There are men like Charlie McNamara, who told Tor and Jane he was never lonely in his remote hut, but, 'I would be lonely if I was in Melbourne.'

COLIN BEARD/WELDON TRANNIES

AUSTRALIAN BROADCASTING CORPORATION

COLIN BEARD

Top and right. *Tor Holth came to the Plains to paint, and became increasingly fascinated by the rough yet comfortable huts which were used by the region's cattlemen.*
Above. *Tor Holth and his wife Jane travelled the Plains widely, painting and writing about the cattlemen and their huts.*

Tor is certainly not the 'bloody city slicker' the high plainsmen first shunned. He says: 'Your word is the most important thing as far as the mountain people are concerned. On it depends whether you struggle along in solitude or you survive in company.' That extremely strong sense of mateship among the cattlemen depends on the strength of their word. Tor counts them all as his best mates.

Much of the Australian Alps and the High Plains are now a national park, with grazing prohibited. Tor and Jane now live on a farm in the foothills of the Great Divide, with two horses, two cattle dogs and two sons.

ONE MAN'S VIEW

Jack Earl has spent most of his life closely involved with canvas. For many people that might mean handling the materials of the world of art, while others might imagine the larger, billowing canvas that is associated with the sea, the wind and sailing ships. To Jack, the word is familiar in both contexts, and it is hard for him to recall which came first — boats or painting. Both interests go far back in his long life. Although he has been successful and highly acclaimed in both of his chosen fields, one day of each year is special. On that day, thousands turn out to watch and participate in the start of Sydney's most exciting event, the Sydney to Hobart yacht race.

Boxing Day, 26 December, is a very special day in the calendar of the yachting fraternity. It is the start of the annual Sydney to Hobart yacht race, one of the world's greatest ocean-racing classics. This is the day when Sydney Harbour is at its most glorious. Excitement fills the air as dozens of racing yachts are accompanied to the Heads by a colourful procession of hundreds of spectator craft of all shapes and sizes. The race itself attracts big names, big yachts and big money, all in order to win a famous prize.

The yachting world is extremely competitive and the stakes are high. Today, renowned yachtsmen such as Dennis Conner and Iain Murray compete in glamorous events such as the America's Cup challenge, and the preparation and financing of such prestigious races is big business. But there was once a different time in the world of yachting, a time when prizes and accolades mattered less, and sailing was, for many, an irresistible and carefree way of life.

Jack Earl remembers those days well; he helped to shape them. It was one of his many adventurous voyages that changed the face of Australian yachting. In 1945 Jack decided to sail from Sydney to Hobart. After six years of war, it seemed an appropriate way to celebrate the new freedom. A couple of his sailing mates, Peter Luke and Bert Walker, thought so too. After consultation with

Above. *Seascape by Jack Earle.*

Opposite. *Yachts vie for position in the few minutes remaining before the Sydney to Hobart yacht race.*

Captain John Illingworth, the English authority on ocean racing, and with the help of the Cruising Yachting Club, the Sydney to Hobart yacht race was created. On 26 December 1945, nine yachts crossed the starting line off the North Head of Sydney Harbour. Today nearly 200 yachts cross the line each year. The race has become an annual blue-water classic that attracts yachts and crews of all sizes from all over the world.

The first Sydney to Hobart race inspired Jack to fulfil his life-long ambition of circumnavigating the world in his yacht *Kathleen*, named after his wife. Jack knew it would be a difficult and dangerous task, but his compulsion was strong. He knew that for eighteen months he would be separated from his wife, and the voyage, apart from obvious dangers, would be a test of the strength of their love. Kathleen understood his obsession: 'Jack is an unusual man, and I was prepared for him to go away. Besides, I believe people should always be individuals, and I do not think that people should have to sacrifice individuality in marriage.'

Understandably, Jack was unhappy to leave Kathleen behind, but found his own unique way of sharing his voyage with her. 'The best I could do was to make her feel as if she were with us; to keep an accurate and detailed logbook for her.' Jack's artistic talents, used in his job as a newspaper illustrator, were to make this more than an ordinary journal or logbook. In addition to describing the voyage, his experiences and fears, the

AUSTRALIAN BROADCASTING CORPORATION

ACTION GRAPHICS

Above. *Jack Earl with one of his paintings.*

Right. *A spectacular view of the annual Sydney to Hobart yacht race.*

AUSTRALIAN BROADCASTING CORPORATION

Jack Earl in his studio. Although now well into his seventies, Jack still paints and sails.

twelve volumes are filled with watercolour drawings and illustrations of scenery, marine life, people and distant ports. Written in the form of letters to Kathleen, the journals are a unique record of a long voyage. For Kathleen, 'They meant everything. As you can imagine, I appreciated the tremendous effort and the love that had gone into them.' It is incredible that Jack found the time and inspiration to complete such a detailed work while navigating the boat and battling rough seas and storms. He even resorted to measures such as mixing his watercolours with salt water in his enthusiasm to sustain the project.

The accounts of Jack's voyage not only brought joy to his wife but also captured the imagination and sentiment of a war-weary country. People throughout Australia enjoyed the romance and adventure of *Kathleen's* departure, travels and eventual return.

Sailing continued to play an important part in Jack Earl's life, but painting began to also make demands upon his time. By the time he was fifty, his paintings were in sufficient demand for Jack to feel confident enough to leave his newspaper job and begin painting full-time. Naturally, the subject of his paintings has

always been that which is closest to his heart and to his experiences. Jack has painted seascapes: boats on wild seas (that have become his trademark), boats at calm anchor on Sydney Harbour, and boats such as Sir Francis Chichester's *Gypsy Moth* rounding Cape Horn during the legendary sailor's single-handed world navigation. If the subject of the painting was not one of personal experience, Jack spent time carefully researching every detail. These paintings are a personal tribute to boats and sailors everywhere and to the spirit that sends men and women to sea, and many of them now hang in galleries around the world.

Both of Jack's interests are demanding, requiring skill, dedication and talent, and his outstanding success in working with both kinds of canvas is a tribute to his ability and persistence. Even though he is now over seventy, Jack still paints and sails, although he finds it increasingly difficult to concentrate on his brushwork for any length of time. But he has faced his ultimate challenge—to paint a scene of the undisturbed elements of sea and sky, with no boats and no men. Jack Earl has achieved much on canvas, both on the sea and with paint.

LA VOLPE

Edgardo Simoni is no longer a young man but his weathered face still reveals the determination, cunning and irreverence which once made him infamous throughout Australia. These qualities gave him the nickname *La Volpe*, The Fox. It was a name given, over forty years ago, as a grudging compliment by those he frustrated, eluded and embarrassed.

In 1942, Edgardo was a handsome young Italian lieutenant, one of the thousands of soldiers captured during the Second World War and brought to Australia for internment in prisoner-of-war camps. While some of the prisoners made unsuccessful efforts to escape, most of them sat out their time resignedly. Edgardo Simoni, however, could not be contained by bars, walls or wire. Through his daring escapes and stealthy evasion of frustrated military and civilian police, Aboriginal trackers and even bloodhounds, he became Australia's most famous and elusive prisoner of war. Even the most massive hunts could not find this fox who constantly fooled, diverted and tricked the hounds that pursued him.

Edgardo's first escape was in June 1942 from the prisoner-of-war camp in the Goulburn Valley, Victoria. He was captured and taken to the prison at Hay, in New South Wales. The authorities believed that this would be the end of the Fox's freedom, but 'They said,' as Edgardo related, '"OK Simoni, we will send you to Hay top security gaol. You certainly will not escape from there." It was a challenge and I took it.'

From his cell at the formidable prison, Edgardo escaped to freedom by filing the window bars for five months and disguising his work by filling the spaces in the mutilated bars with soap. The filing made a suspicious noise which Edgardo managed to cover up by singing. Making this excuse to the guards, he innocently apologised, 'I am sorry boys, sometimes I have to sing at night-time.'

As he sang and filed, Edgardo thought of the day when he would be free. That day arrived on 23 November 1943, leaving the prison authorities astounded by his escape from their stronghold. Guards had checked Edgardo's cell on the night he had escaped, but he left a dummy in his bed to fool them — the trick he was to repeat many times during the next few months. For now, the cunning Fox was free again.

Edgardo Simoni had a well thought out plan. He would follow the banks of the Murrumbidgee River to the point where it joined the Murray. Edgardo hoped that the community of Italian farmers living there would help him, but he could not be sure of this as Italians were under suspicion during the war and many were imprisoned or under surveillance. They were therefore reluctant to take the risk.

ST 1233 n3   1877[56] 1

ST 1233 n3   1877[56] 2

Mug shots of Edgardo Simoni:
Australia's most elusive wartime escapee.

CARMEN KY

*Simoni's escape route from Hay prison in New South Wales lay along
the banks of the Murrumbidgee River.*

CARMEN KY

Some of the Victorian countryside that the Fox would have covered in his bid to avoid being caught by the police.

Fortunately for Edgardo, Dominic Di Pietro was prepared to take that risk. All went well until someone informed the authorities that the Fox was in the area. Di Pietro's house received a dawn visit from the local police, but Edgardo remained calm and did not panic. He stayed in his bed and pulled the sheets over his head, while Di Pietro fooled the police into believing that it was his brother who was asleep in the bed.

After this narrow escape, it was time for Edgardo to move on. He made his way to Melbourne, often eluding his pursuers by hiding in trees as they rode by below. Even when he was sick with a fever, he managed not to get caught but moved, unrecognised, through twenty-five towns, forging documents and learning English in his bid to stay free.

He learned his new language well, in fact so well that by the time he reached Melbourne he was able to take a job as a door-to-door salesman. Assuming the name of George Scotto, Edgardo was convincing enough to be named salesman of the month. For two months in the very heart of the city and still unrecognised, he spent his days chatting with and charming housewives with his talk of the products he was selling.

Why did no one recognise him? As Edgardo explained, 'They had no photo of me because in the camp I sent somebody else to be photographed in my place, so when the photo appeared in the newspapers, it was not me.' This was a clever fox, clever and cheeky enough to share a beer with a local policeman, confident in the belief that he would not be caught. Even so, Edgardo's instinct told him that it was time for him to leave the city. He knew that 'Melbourne was risky again. I smelt a rat — some danger to me — and I went to Mildura to pick grapes.'

After grape-picking, Edgardo went back along the Murrumbidgee River, stole a boat and spent his days enjoying the river that he liked so much. He had a narrow escape there but, yet again the Fox eluded the authorities by diving overboard and disappearing into the bush. The authorities were totally frustrated by the cunning of this man. All attempts to find him had failed — ten months and thousands of kilometres later, Edgardo was still free. To the repressed Italian community he became a hero and a symbol of the freedom they lacked.

But even a fox eventually runs out of luck, and La Volpe's luck ran out with a chance encounter with a young policeman. The young policeman spotted a suspicious looking man in the bush and chased him, unaware of the importance of the prize he was about to catch. On capturing Edgardo, the policeman was mystified by the man's reaction. 'When I got to the tree,' the policeman recalled, 'somebody ran away from it. I chased him and caught him and while I was sitting on his chest, he was singing out — "Gee, you're lucky".' This was the end of the Fox's long run.

Edgardo stayed on in Australia for another year after Italy's surrender. Years later, he visited Australia to relive his great escapes and adventures. The taste of freedom he believes is all the more thrilling when you have to fight for it, and *La Volpe* — Edgardo Simoni — knows that feeling better than most people. 'I'd like many people to have the chance to feel in the same way, in some moment of their lives, free.'

MASTER OF HIS TRADE

Sugar is a product that we all enjoy in one form or another, but as we spoon the white crystals into our morning cup of tea or coffee, how many of us stop to think of either the cane from which it comes, or the workers who labour to produce it?

Sugar cane has been grown commercially for a long time in Australia. The first enterprise began over a hundred years ago in the green and fertile Macleay and Clarence Rivers region of northern New South Wales, later spreading to north Queensland. Today, cane is grown in many parts of the world, but Australia has been the only country where European people have laboured in the cane fields. From 1863 until 1906 Pacific Islanders — known as 'kanakas' — were brought to work in the cane fields. Since then this hard, back-breaking work has been done by Europeans.

Working conditions remained the same until recently, when machinery took over much of the cane cutting process, and the tough cane cutters began to disappear. Cane cutters are a special breed — resilient, hard working and greatly respected by the growers who employ them. Their work is tough. In the old days men

laboured from dawn till dusk but more recently the hours have been shortened to a still punishing eight-hour day. Cutters contend with heat, sweat, ash and smoke from fires, and sometimes even their own blood on the cane. They even encounter snakes that inhabit the densely packed cane fields. Nevertheless, there has always been pride in the work. As one cutter states, 'It is one of the few things in Australia you can do with your hands, but you really sweat, and I mean sweat!'

For a century little changed in the cane-cutting process. Men toiled with their wide bladed knives — hacking and trimming and cutting, and firing their fields. In the early days the fields were fired not only to rid the fields of snakes and rats, but also to strip the cane of its leaves, as cutters used to carry the loads of cane on their shoulders. The introduction of mechanical loaders ended this need for stripping, but the hot and dirty work of firing continued. Also, while machines such as loaders eased the punishing work, the cutting itself was still a strenuous task that demanded a great deal from the men who worked to feed the hungry sugar mills. As a long-time cutter said: 'It is asking a bit much to ask the

This genteel depiction of sugar-cane cutting on the Clarence River, northern New South Wales, appeared in the Illustrated Sydney News, *10 February 1875.*

Top and above. *Until the relatively recent introduction of labour-saving cutting and loading machinery, sugar-cane cutters had to endure back-breaking conditions.*

younger generation to cut cane now — when we have men on the moon — because it is extremely hard work. We cannot ask people to come out and sweat and toil like the old cane cutters used to.'

Attitudes have altered and machinery has changed the nature of the work, but men have always been drawn to cane cutting, for both monetary reasons, and the pride of doing a hard job well. The leader, or ganger, drives his men hard to bring in the big money. Wes Johnson is a ganger on the Clarence River fields. He pushes his four cutters to work at a frantic pace, leading them to produce an amazing 25 tonnes of cut cane each day.

Apart from the hard work, there is an art to cutting cane, and all new recruits are given a chance to learn the ropes, and prove that they can work quickly. There has never been any room for slackers in this line of work. During the trial period, an experienced cutter explained, 'You must have equal men. You cannot have anyone not doing his thing, not keeping up. It is different if you have a new man in the gang and he is doing his best to keep up. Well you usually give him a go — a few weeks or a month, or whatever the gang thinks, to come up to scratch. If he does not come up to scratch, well, he just has to leave.'

During the crushing season both the fields and the mills are a hive of activity. The mill works day and night to crush the cane and turn it into sugar and by-products such as molasses. It takes 7 to 9 tonnes of cane to produce one tonne of sugar and the men have to keep up with the vast appetite of the mill. It is to those men's credit that they always keep pace and even somehow enjoy what most people would regard as unpleasant physical work. As one cane cutter summed it up, 'It is like a disease. As soon as the season starts, your mind is with the men and the field. I stayed home two seasons in the last sixteen or seventeen years and I could not stop thinking of the men in the cane!'

The day of the cane cutter may have almost gone, but these are special men, a different breed. As one grower said, 'A cane cutter has no equal throughout the world. In fact, he is the master of his trade.'

Right. *At sugar mills such as this one at Proserpine, Queensland, cane cutters have to work long hours. It takes 7 to 9 tonnes of cane to produce just one tonne of sugar, and the workers have to keep up with the mills' voracious appetites.*

Overleaf. *Cane firing is a spectacular and dramatic sight. Firing originated as a means of stripping the cane of its leaves, as well as ridding the fields of pests such as rats and snakes. Even though stripping is now done mechanically, cane cutters still have to pursue the hot, dirty task of firing.*
REG MORRISON/WELDON TRANNIES

RAY JOYCE/WELDON TRANNIES

YOUNG TOM

Far from the noise and pollution of Australia's towns and cities, Mountain River Valley nestles into the hills of southern Tasmania. It is a wilderness of tall straight trees in ageless forests; a land of streams, hills and verdant grasslands.

Pioneers came to the valley over 140 years ago. They came for the abundant timber, to build their houses and to farm the land. Among those hardy and determined settlers was the Brown family who made timber-getting their work, and who began a long association with the valley that has stretched uninterrupted through five generations.

Young Tom Brown is a glowing advertisement for the fortitude of these five generations. A shock of blonde hair frames a rosy-cheeked face that exudes country freshness and good health. Tom was never particularly interested in study, but, unlike the other four Brown children, he is interested in following the long tradition of his family. He willingly left school at thirteen to work with his father, Darryl, as the only employee in the small family timber business. Darryl, who was only twelve when he began working at the mill, thinks that Tom has missed little by leaving school: 'He might as well be here learning something practical than at school learning nothing. There are too many bludgers around now. If he has to work a little bit, he will be far better off. I would say that he is more educated than other boys of his age '

Despite offers to purchase his property by large companies, Darryl is determined to keep the small and no longer profitable mill in operation. He is teaching Tom every detail of the trade he knows so well, to prepare him for the inevitability of joining a large operation. The days of the small mill are numbered as big timber companies battle for quotas of forest that leave little for small operators like the Browns. Darryl and Tom call themselves salvage timber-getters. They reap the smaller trees that are ignored by the big mills, and still try to maintain the family's longstanding reputation for quality.

It is not easy to make a living in this way. In Darryl's youth, when the mill was profitable, the trees stretched throughout Mountain River Valley and the pick of the timber was at the Browns' doorstep. They fashioned the apple boxes into which the fruits of the valley were packed and shipped to many destinations. Now the apple orchards have gone, and so, for Darryl and Tom, has most of the timber. They must drive 40 kilometres daily to the Russell River Valley to fell what little they can find in the forest. Among the moss, ferns and lush undergrowth they search for myrtle, celery pine and black heart sassafras.

Timber-cutting is an arduous job with long hours, but Tom and his father are mates and work well together, usually in contented silence. In a land where men are judged by their strength and courage, Tom is obviously making the grade after the first year of his apprenticeship. According to Darryl 'He is not very old yet, but he is coming along fine with what he has done. He has made a go of it and he has gone from strength to strength.' This is high praise indeed from a taciturn man such as Darryl.

Grandfather Reg approves too. Despite his grey hair, he is still regarded as the strongest man in the valley and is evidently delighted that young Tom has chosen to follow in his and Darryl's footsteps. All three men take pride in their strength and test this in the seemingly childish pursuits of wielding a four-kilo mallet and attempting to lift an unsuspecting horse. To these men this is not childishness but a test of their manhood. Tom's mother Bev thinks otherwise and often scolds them for their silliness.

AUSTRALIAN BROADCASTING CORPORATION

Young Tom and his father Darryl at work in the forest.
Opposite:
Top. *The Browns' Tasmanian timber mill.*
Bottom. *Tom Brown is the last in a long line of timber cutters. For him, change is inevitable.*

Bev is the archetypal country woman and mother. Her days are spent in preparing food, cooking, serving, washing up, and then repeating the process — three times a day. It is her responsibility to feed the family large and wholesome quantities of food to ensure that they maintain their strength for the physical work they perform. Bev willingly accepts this role, and the family acknowledges her important contribution to the team.

Out at the mill, the only one remaining in the area, Tom and Darryl saw, chop and stack the timber. It is an important part of the process of understanding the material that they work with, and Tom is learning all that his father knows. They make this work look easy, but as Darryl says, 'There is an art to it. It's like everything else, if you are going to make a success at something, you have to know what you are doing.'

Most of the houses in the valley have been built with the Browns' timber, and their wood is still sold as planks and beams to the small community. The offcuts are sold as firewood: nothing is wasted, especially in times like this when timber is hard to come by.

The Browns are an integral part of Mountain River Valley — the descendants of those men and women who came and toiled, as Reg and Darryl and Tom still do, for the timber. It has always been a tough life, but, as Darryl says, 'I reckon it is a pretty hard way of making a living, but when there is not much offering and you have to find work for yourself and your boy, well you have to do something. Beggars can't be choosers.'

Beggars cannot be choosers: this is the crisis that the Brown family now faces. There is not much timber left for the small operator, and for young Tom especially, change is in the mountain air. He is the latest in the line of five timber-getting generations and it seems certain that he will be the first to be forced to leave the valley to pursue his family trade. A tradition of 140 years will be broken, and though change has come slowly to Mountain River Valley, this change, for young Tom at least, is inevitable.

JOHN M. VOGEL/WELDON TRANNIES

Above and opposite. *Thousands of people each year attempt to run the City to Surf but few will attempt the gruelling distance of a marathon.*

Of all the varied and exciting track-and-field athletic events, none seems to capture the public's imagination more than the longest race of all — the marathon. From its ancient Greek origins to the present day, the event has provoked much discussion and excitement among athletics fans. It may not be the most glamorous race, but it is certainly the most gruelling, requiring stamina and endurance far beyond the capabilities of most people. To run the distance of more than 42 kilometres in a little over two hours is an incredible task, and it takes no ordinary athlete to achieve this goal.

Robert de Castella is one such unusual man. Affectionately known as 'Deek' by the Australian public and press, he has always had running in his blood. In 1975 he was his school's athletics captain, and, though beaten in many races, his love for the sport kept him on the track. He eventually began competing in the greatest race of all, the marathon, becoming Australia's best and most famous long distance runner.

The Brisbane Commonwealth Games in 1982 gave Deek the chance to prove himself in front of his home crowd. Rated as the world's second fastest marathon runner, and buoyed by a great victory in Japan, the twenty-five-year-old biophysicist felt confident that he could succeed. Watched by the Commonwealth Games

spectators in Brisbane and millions of television viewers in Australia and around the world, he was taking on the Commonwealth's best, including Juma Ikaanga and Gidamis Shahanga, the two formidable runners from the African country of Tanzania. Together, these three men were to turn the race into a nail-biting episode of athletics drama.

The race began on a steamy spring morning, with humidity levels up to a distressing 94 per cent — hardly ideal conditions for such a long race. Despite Deek's confidence he was run down and tired, suffering from a strained back and lack of sleep. Understandably his wife, Gayelene, also a distance runner, and his coach Pat Clohessy, were worried. As they watched, Deek and the other entrants pounded the Brisbane roads and streets, with the two Tanzanians taking an anticipated early lead. This suited Deek well; on a humid day like this he preferred to follow in their shadow, although he intended to take the lead later.

As the humidity increased and Deek was forced to accept drinks and wet sponges from each wayside station, the incredible Tanzanians raced on without stopping. By now, Deek was almost a minute behind the white, green and gold-clad African pair. On the street, Gayelene waited anxiously for a view of her third-placed

husband. At this stage Deek was running alone, unable to bring the trailing pack up to his pace, and still well behind the out-of-sight front runners. On one of the hills, Deek ran into more trouble. Stomach cramps and diarrhoea struck as he struggled through an unforgettably painful 700 metres of road.

One of the trade marks of the marathon runner is persistence and, almost miraculously, spurred on by the patriotic crowd, Deek closed on the second-placed runner, Shahanga. Australians everywhere watched their television screens with bated breath as Deek finally caught and passed the Tanzanian. The race was now in its final stages and Deek and the leader, Ikaanga, battled for over a kilometre to lead the race as they passed, followed and repassed each other in a desperate and exciting contest. Ikaanga had led throughout and was now tiring. Sensing this, Deek finally took the undisputed lead just a few kilometres from the finish.

For the courageous Australian, the final stage was a matter of gritting his teeth and battling on. With tired legs and no idea of how far ahead he was, he just kept up his steady pace, and, to the frantic cheers of Gayelene, his coach and the enormous crowd, he finished first. He had won! Ikaanga came in just 12 seconds later — the fastest time ever run by an African and a very narrow margin in terms of a marathon. His was a great achievement, but the day undoubtedly belonged to Australia's Robert de Castella. His will and endurance had defeated the humidity, a bad back, stitch, diarrhoea and stomach cramps, as well as the best runners that the Commonwealth could offer.

In two hours, nine minutes and eighteen seconds, Deek had run 42 kilometres and beaten all opposition in a tightly fought and exciting race. The legendary runner, Ron Clarke, called the race 'the greatest marathon ever run', and Deek's evident delight was shared by proud Australians throughout the country. He simply said of his remarkable win, 'I had no choice.' As he stepped on to the podium to receive his gold medal, it was another great moment in a glittering marathon career.

Robert de Castella won the prestigious Boston marathon in 1987.

Index

Aboriginal art galleries, 206
Aboriginal art, modern, 166–71, 174–76
Aboriginal people in modern society, 204–07
Aborigines, Tasmanian, 68
Addison, Harry, 188–89
Amer, Patrick, 124–25, 129
Anemone fish, 98
Anemone, tube, 24
Anemones, sea, 94–98, 100–01
Angler fish, 24, 26
Ants, Green tree, 89
Araluen Arts Centre, Alice Springs, 167

Bardon, Geoff, 166
Barker, Alan, 189
Barton, David, 90, 93
Bates, Daisy, 36
Batik, 174-77
Bats, Fruit, 53, 58
Bear, The (horse), 214–15
Berry, Tony, 189
Bethune, Neal, 69, 75
Billinudgel, New South Wales, 187–89
Bird, Eileen, *Wild orange and centipede awelye,* 177
Biscuit star, 30–31
Bogong High Plains, Victoria, 216–19
Booby, Abbott's, 40
Bourke, Frank, 178–79
Briggs, John, 20, 22
Brown, Darryl, 234–35
Brown, Tom, 234–35
Brumbies, 134, 136–37, 138
Brush turkey, 53, 58
Buffalo, 140–42, 145

Campbell, Donald, 112
Cape Barren goose, 64, 66, 67
Caterpillars, 82, 84–85
Chandra, Ram, 201–03
Christmas Island (Indian Ocean), 38–40
Circumcision ritual, 159
City to surf race, 196–97
Claypans, 114–15
Coral fan, Red, 28–29
Corals, 26–27, 94, 100
Correspondence education, 194–95
Crab, Christmas Island red, 40
Crab, Decorator, 30, 94, 102–03
Croll, Ian, 120
Cruise, Noel, 131

Daintree rainforest, Queensland, 54–57
Darwinia, 22
de Castella, Robert, 237–39
Decorator crab, 30, 94, 102–03
Drivers (musterers), 139–45
Dryandra, 20, 22
Dulhunty, John, 112, 116
Dulhunty, Roma, 112, 116

Earl, Jack, 220–24
Eighteen-footer yachts, 152–55
Eyre, Edward John, 32
Eyre, Lake, 112–16

Fairy penguins, 90–93
False killer whales, 75
Feather star, 24, 30–31
Ferris, Tony, 139, 142
Fig, Strangler, 50
Flatworms, 26
Flavell, Ian, 61
Flies (tropical), 88
Flinders Island, Tasmania, 65, 66
Flying Fish Cove, Christmas Island, 38
Forrest, John, 32, 36
Foy, Mark, 152
Frigate bird, Greater, 39
Fruit bats, 53, 58
Furneaux Group, Tasmania, 64–68
Furneaux, Tobias, 64

G.W. Wolf (wreck), 68
Gannet, Australian, 67
Gannet, Cape, 64
George (raft), 124–29
Giles, Ernest, 32
Gliding, 121–23
Goombala, Ian, 204
Gordon River, Tasmania 46–47, 49
Great Australian Bight, 36
Great Barrier Reef, 100

Harvester judgment, 192
Hawk-owl, Christmas Island, 39
Hawkmoth caterpillar, 82
Hays, Brickie, 61
Helicopter mustering, 139–45
Hepworth, John, 124–25, 129
Hindle, John, 124–25, 129
Holth, Jane, 216, 218
Holth, Tor, 216–19
Horsemen, high country, 110-11, 134–38
Hotham, Mount, Victoria, 76
Hume, Lake, 124
Huon pines, 49

Insect eating plants, 82, 83, 86–87
Insecticides, effect of, on the ecology, 87–88
Insects, 80–89
Itinerant teachers, 194–95

Jamieson, Don, 76
Japandawa, Albert, 204
Jewel beetle, 62–63
Jones, Spencer, 189
Juddamurra, Michael Nelson, 168
Junee, New South Wales, 146–47

Kakadu community school, 205
Kngwarreye, Ruby, *Blue tongue lizard awelye,* 176
Kunoth-Monks, Rosalie, 174, 177

La Volpe (Edgardo Simoni), 225–27
Lemonthyme Forest, Tasmania, 18–19
Leschenaultia, 22–23
Levy, Laurie, 69, 75
Litjens, Hans, 130

McGovern, John, 149–51
McKay, Hugh, 190–93
McTavish, Bob, 208, 212
Maralinga, South Australia, 36
Marine life, 24–31, 94–103
Matupit Island, Rabaul, 43
Merbein, Victoria, 129
Monte Cristo, Junee, 146–47
Mountain pygmy possum, 76–79
Mullaring, Nelson, 207
Murray, River, 124–29
Mustering by helicopter, 139–45
Muttonbirds, 64

New Brighton Hotel, Billinudgel, 188–89
Nullarbor plain, 32–37
Numbat, 104–09

O'Donnell, Ian, 149–51
Octopus, 31, 99

Papunya, Northern Territory, 166–71
Paulius, Nason, 43, 45
Pedder, Lake, Tasmania, 46
Pendergast family, 134–35, 138
Penguins, Fairy, 90–93
Peppimenarti, Northern Territory, 158–65
Persson, Bert, 122
Petyarre, Anna, *Emu hunt and wild tomato awelye,* 174
Phosphate mining, 38, 40
Pilot whale, Long-finned, 69
Pitcher plant, 83, 87
Potter, Martin, 209
Praying mantis, 80–81
Pygmy possum, mountain, 76–79

Queenstown, Tasmania, 49
Quinkan rock art, 172–73

Rabaul, Papua New Guinea, 41–45
Rainforests, Australian, 50–59
Red-tailed tropic bird, 39, 40
Renner, Ingo, 121–22
Richardson, Ray, 61
Riley, Bill, 121–22
Ring, Margaret Alice, 187–88
Roughsey, Dick, 172–73
Roycroft, Vicki, 214–15
Ryan, Olive, 146–47
Ryan, Reg, 146–47

Samuels, Jeffery, 205
Sapphire mining, 60–61
Sapphire, Queensland, 60–61
Sea hare, 26
Sea slug (nudibranch), 30
Sea slug, batwing, 26, 94
Seal hunting in Bass Strait, 64, 66
Sharks, 117–20
Shipwrecks in Bass Strait, 66, 68
Short board (surf), 208–09, 212
Shortman, Ken, 76
Simoni, Edgardo, 225–27
Sims, Colleen, 194–95
Sims, Frank, 194–95
Sky, Ron, 60–61
Snail, Giant, 58
Snakes (rainforest), 59
Sorsby, Bill, 187–88
Sovereign Hill, Ballarat, 180–86
Spring, Bob, 189
Starfish, 24, 30–31
Stirling Ranges, Western Australia, 21
Stokes, Tony, 40
Strangler fig, 50
Sturt's desert pea, 162
Sugar cane cutting, 228–33
Sugar mill, Proserpine, Queensland, 230–31
Sundew, 86-87
Sunshine Harvester, 190–93
Surfboard riding, 208–13
Sydney Cove (wreck), 68
Sydney to Hobart yacht race, 220, 222–23

Taipan, 201–03
Talai, Benjamin, 43
Tasmania, southwestern, 46–49
Termite hills, Northern Territory, 82
Termites, 88
Terns, White-fronted, 66
Tiger shark, 117, 118–19
Timber cutting in Tasmania, 234–35
Tjampitjinpa, Maxie, 168, 170
Tjampitjinpa, Nelson, 170
Trezise, Percy, 172–73
Tropic bird, Red-tailed, 39, 40
Truchanas, Olegas, 46–49
Tulau, Greg, 210–211
Turkey, Brush, 53, 58
Tyrell, Rex, 150–51

Ultra lights (aircraft), 130–33
Utopia, Nothern Territory, 174–77

Venus flytrap, 82, 87
Volcanic eruptions in Rabaul, 42, 45

Walton, Nancy Bird, 198–200
Water tank caravan, 116
Western Australian native plants, 20–23
Weymouth, John, 139
Whale Research Centre, Melbourne, 69, 75
Whale strandings, 69–75
White-fronted terns, 66
White Rose Orchestra, 178–79
Williams, Don, 20–22

Yachts, Eighteen-footer, 152–55

Zanoni (wreck), 148–51